N*you*ever
K now
L*your*uck

Reflections of a cockney campaigner for education

Fred Jarvis

**Grosvenor House
Publishing Limited**

The right of Fred Jarvis to be identified as the author of this
work has been asserted by him in accordance with Section 78
of the Copyright, Designs and Patents Act 1988

The book cover picture is copyright to Fred Jarvis

This book is published by
Grosvenor House Publishing Ltd
28-30 High Street, Guildford, Surrey, GU1 3EL.
www.grosvenorhousepublishing.co.uk

Front cover photo:
Fred Jarvis welcoming the Queen to the NUT's National Education
and Careers Exhibition at Olympia in 1959.

Back cover:
Nelson Mandela at the Labour Party conference.
Poppies in Claude Monet's garden at Giverny.
The Mayor and *vignerons* of Ste Cécile.
Simon Rattle conducting "the world's largest orchestra".
All the photographs in this book which do not include
Fred Jarvis were taken by the author.

The author wishes to thank The Trustees for the Copyright of Dylan Thomas
for permission to include the "Song" by Dylan Thomas in this book.
It is published this year (2014) by Orion in John Goodby's new edition of
The Complete Poems of Dylan Thomas.

A CIP record for this book
is available from the British Library

ISBN 978-1-78148-723-5

To my family and my friends

Contents

Foreword

We cockney kids used to have a reputation for cheeky repartee. Well, at least Max Miller did, but then he probably wasn't a cockney, just a "cheeky chappie". But I have a feeling that kind of repartee is not altogether appropriate in a foreword to one's first (and probably only) book.

But to put it succinctly (which is not my normal style, as those who heard me in teachers' pay negotiations would certainly testify), I am still too much in awe of the universe to be frivolous. Looking at those marvellous television programmes about the universe and space travel by Brian Cox and the geeks of NASA, I find myself left utterly in awe by what they are describing or showing on the television screen. Staggered by the sheer vastness and age of it all, one is left with a sense of the total insignificance of human beings. And then there are those programmes about plans being made to launch missions to Mars – when of course what is needed is the political will to spend the resources needed to get to Mars on tackling the problems in our own backyard.

Then, after all the awe and bewilderment that these programmes produce, you look away from the television and cast your eye around the room and you begin to think that, for all our insignificance, what has happened and is happening here on Earth is fantastic in itself. In relative terms, in the context of our own planet, we are not insignificant and even though we're only here for a couple of seconds (relatively speaking) there's a lot to do, much to be strived for and achieved if we have the wherewithal to do it.

From all of which you will have realised that this isn't a book about space science or philosophy, although this foreword does suggest what can happen if you look at the telly as you ponder what you might say in introducing a book which is concerned, far too much maybe, with one's own journey through life – on Earth.

Although I have spoken of our insignificance when measured against the immensity of the universe we have, or should have, the possibility to become significant as individuals, each and every one of us. We didn't apply to become members of the human race, we're here courtesy of somebody else; but once we're here we should have the opportunity to benefit from the ingenuity and creativity of men and women of today, and throughout history. And the principal key to the enjoyment of those opportunities is education.

Of course it's not the only means of access – in many, but not all respects, having the resources to pay for access is vital. Again, education is a principal means of access, and one of the gross injustices of our society is how such access is still denied to so many. And that is why education should be seen as, and must become, a liberating force.

I get tired of those politicians who talk as if social mobility is the main aim of education. For they are often the very politicians whose policies create the barriers to mobility in the first place. They are the ones who foster the inequalities that leave so many at the bottom of the pile or the foot of the ladder. I want education to produce citizens who will seek to break down the barriers and remove the possibility of a minority climbing up the ladder at the expense of their fellow citizens. But I do not believe that some of those who talk about social mobility as the aim of education have that in mind. Their philosophy is generally one which, as I said of Mrs Thatcher in my presidential address to the TUC, is that of putting self first and pulling up the ladder once they are on board.

By all means, let us look seriously at all the factors that lead to the disadvantage and underachievement that affect so many children and young people; and let us recognise that to overcome this is a very complex and also a very costly task which will not be solved only by "pupil premiums". Let us not be misled either by those who measure the success of a school by the number of places its pupils secure at Oxford or Cambridge, an absurd yardstick to apply. As I say below, I immensely enjoyed my time at Oxford, but I would not insult all the other universities and colleges by implying that they have not great qualities and opportunities to offer.

I hope my opinions on such matters (and I have them on quite a few others too) will show why I have felt it so important to campaign about education, its funding and provision, over so many years, and why I am so grateful to all those who have enabled me to play my part and all those who have worked and campaigned with me.

I was very moved when Tony Benn, interviewed on television, said he was not afraid of death. I don't think I could ever be that brave. And I've not yet got to the point when I want to say "stop the world, I want to get off". There are still so many things I would love to do. And I do not want to get off the education bus, even if it is in danger of being driven over a cliff by an obsessed ideologue. There is too much at stake, too much that has happened in education to be grateful for, too much that still needs doing.

Given that virtually the whole of my working life has been spent in education, much of this book relates to events and developments in education, in some of which I have been directly involved. But my involvement has not been that of a teacher or educationist – I have taught very few. I have certainly addressed lots of audiences and meetings, large and small, and education events, but it has been as a campaigner for education and for those who provide it and receive it, or who should get more of it than they already receive.

St Mary's C of E primary school in Manchester's Moss Side, is an outstanding school in which 80% of the children are in receipt of free school meals and 75% have English as a second language. On one of my visits there, one of the pupils, Rayan Farouk, asked me "what is it like to be a union boss?" Rayan is a Somali and only ten years old, but clearly has already absorbed the language of the anti-trade union media to whom trade union leaders are either "bosses" or "barons" (usually barons). I told Rayan that I never felt like a "boss" when I was general secretary of the NUT. For me, my role was that of leader of a team of people dedicated to meeting the needs and wishes of the many thousands of members whose subscription paid our salaries, and whose aims and aspirations, set out in the decisions of the union's conference and executive, laid down the framework of our responsibilities. I've no doubt that every union general secretary or chief executive has his or her own way of discharging those responsibilities, but to suggest as sections of the media often do that they act like all-powerful "barons" (or worse) is a grotesque caricature. As I said in my presidential address to the TUC, invariably their main concerns are how to persuade more members to play an active part in the union, to express their views on the union's policies and to convey their needs and concerns.

Well, that's a longer answer than I gave my Somali questioner, but it embodies what I felt about my job and how I saw my role as general secretary of the NUT. And to be fair to the many journalists and broadcasters with whom I had contact over so many years, quite often they said kind things about me. For example, the *Observer* said: "...immensely cheerful, energetic and shrewd. He is an uncomplicated man of great warmth, with a relish for life, without a trace of pretension or bitterness, utterly at ease with himself." And for the *Sunday Times* I was "lovable, dedicated and dependable, rather like a latter-day Mr Chips. Teachers feel safe with Fred. They like a man who... has the courage to be himself, who eschews the smoothness of the media whizz-kids."

I've no doubt that plenty of less kind things have also been said in some quarters, but whether they have or not I greatly enjoyed most of my time with the union and am immensely grateful for all the opportunities and challenges it gave me. I guess it was those opportunities and challenges which greatly contributed to what the friends who encouraged me to write this book have said has been my "interesting life".

I think these pages will show that my work for the union has not been the whole of my life and that a passionate interest in and devotion to the cause of education has not been my only concern and activity. I've been fortunate to be able to pursue a range of interests and passions, all of them enjoyable and, to some extent, fulfilling: my involvement in politics, photography, the football and horse-racing, the arts, the concert-going, the foreign travel, the "second life" in Provence, the now thwarted love of books and, above all, the continuing love of my family and of so many dear friends. It all adds up to a powerful reason for not wanting to stop the world and get off.

And it won't escape notice that at various points along the road of life I've had a slice of luck, and no more so than when, as I neared the end of my war service, I was sent for training to serve in military government in the quiet backwaters of Schleswig Holstein and not sent to Burma, as my best mate was, to endure more war and suffer ill-health.

There has also been at least one of those "what if" moments. In my case "what if" I had accepted the post I had been offered to become the director of communications at the newly opened Open University? A fine education enterprise of great credit to a Labour government, it has developed as a tremendous benefit to countless thousands of adults, many of whom were in need of a second chance to obtain higher education. Had I joined its staff I guess my career would have developed in a very different way to that which I had with the NUT. It has been very gratifying to know that while I did not take the post at the Open University, my daughter Jacky, having been awarded a PhD by the OU, then joined its academic staff for more than 20 years, becoming a senior lecturer before going on to become a deputy dean at Northampton University Business School.

And to look at another "what if" speculation: what if I had won Wallasey for Labour in the 1951 general election instead of losing by 15,000 votes? Well, that possibility was so remote that such speculation is pure fantasy. It was even less likely to happen than winning a Barnet Council seat for the borough's richest ward, Totteridge, when I stood there as a "paper" candidate for Labour on two occasions.

Back from the realm of fantasy, I do want to say how grateful I am to those who have helped me to publish this, my first book. First, those friends who urged me to "write a book". I will not name them individually, lest any of them are embarrassed by the end result, but without their encouragement I would not have dreamed of writing this volume.

Having decided to take the plunge, I would not have been able to write the book without the tremendous help I have had from my son, Robin. He has typed every word and, fortunately, he is able to read my handwriting better than I can myself. Not only that, but he has also made many helpful suggestions along the way. My gratitude to him is enormous.

I am especially grateful to my friends and former colleagues, Toni Griffiths, who has helped and advised me throughout the project, and Peter Singer, who has been a wise and very supportive editor. I am also very grateful for the help I have had from my former colleagues Graham Clayton and Barry Fawcett, and from Janet Friedlander, the NUT's excellent information officer, whose unrivalled knowledge of the union's archives and records has been invaluable in refreshing my sometimes hazy memory of events over the past 60 years.

I wish also to thank my friends Godfrey Smith, Ed Dorrell, Will Woodward and Ann Corbett, who have helped and encouraged me from the outset. While the advice and help of all these friends and others is greatly appreciated, I wish to make it clear that the responsibility for any opinions expressed in these pages is mine and mine alone. Although I say "you never know your luck", I do know there is one piece of luck I have had and continue to enjoy – and that is having so many dear and kind friends, most of whom have shared in one or more aspects of my life in education recalled in these pages.

Fred Jarvis
May 2014

Part 1: Formative times

The early years

I suppose it would be called stalking nowadays, but at the time it did not feel like that. All I knew was that I had a crush on Lillian Tindall, a blonde in the year above me at "Plaistow Sec", and there she was, alone and on her way home, going the same way as me, so there was a chance that if I could catch up with her I might be able to engage her in conversation on some pretext or other. But Hitler had other ideas. Just as I was getting closer to Lillian, the air raid sirens howled their warning and a woman in the house I was passing urged me to come into their air-raid shelter. So Lillian, or rather I, would have to wait until another day. Within minutes there was a bomber overhead and not long afterwards the sound of a bomb exploding – in the direction of the road where I lived. The "all clear" could not come quickly enough for I was worried that my mother would be very anxious when I did not get home at the usual time.

I thanked my "shelterers" and rushed off home, with no sign of Lillian, and soon reached the spot where the bomb had fallen – in the road next to ours. It hadn't hit any houses and already people were coming to stare at the crater. It was the first bomb to fall on the East End since the war had begun, so their curiosity was understandable. But the following day that curiosity would turn to fear as it proved to be the day the Blitz would begin in earnest. That night, as we huddled together in our own shelter, we could hear the sound of pounding feet as those living nearer the docks made their escape to what they hoped would be the safety of Wanstead Flats.

That episode was the most dramatic in my early years, overriding memories of the elusive Lillian (who later became an actress on BBC radio) who was soon to be replaced in my aspiring affections by the lovely Irene Beecham. I had to say a reluctant farewell to Irene too when we were obliged to move to Wallasey (in my case virtually kicking and screaming at the prospect) because the flour mill where my father worked had been burnt down: he was transferred to a disused mill in Birkenhead which was reopened to maintain production.

Up to that point my early years had been happy and undisturbed, but I do not remember as much about them as I would have liked. At my age I suppose that it is not altogether surprising. (How much do you remember of yours, may I ask?) If I could remember better it would enable me to say in more detail how much my parents did for me and my brother, Dennis, and how grateful I am for all that they did. I envy those who have written at length about being brought up in the East End but, if my memory is less vivid than theirs, my main recollection is that as a family we shared many good things, and faced none of the hardships that so many of those around us encountered.

In spite of my general failure to remember more, there are nevertheless odd things that stick in the memory from those distant days. Things like eating jellied eels and pie and mash in Stratford (which I still do when I go to football at Upton Park); watching the vendor of cats' meat, pannier on his back, being followed by a string of cats past our house; waiting on Sunday afternoons for the cart selling cockles and shrimps, whelks and winkles; getting pease pudding and faggots at the pork butcher across the road from the Apollo, the fleapit cinema where we watched Buck Jones and Tom Mix; the taste of coffee we drank for the first time in Paris on our 1938 school trip; and those bath nights, when the signature tune of *In Town Tonight* brought London's traffic to a halt, and we took it in turns to step into the tin bath in the scullery, filled with hot water from the copper. Who could ever forget that tune?

Then there were the trips to Barking Creek to see a friend who had a boat there on which he was always working but never sailed; and bunking in for free at West Ham stadium to watch the thrills and spills of speedway racing and getting the autographs of favourite riders like Bluey Wilkinson, Tommy Coombs, Max Groskreutz and Lionel van Praag. And in those days, I clearly recall, more carts and horses than lorries and cars came down our streets, which meant that we could (fairly) safely play cricket in them using lamp posts as wickets, trundle our marbles along the gutters and shoot balls of varying size into the goal chalked on the wall of the corner shop whose owner used to sell milk, hopefully not curdled, from an open churn. Across the road from us a haulier named Cook had a yard with carts and sturdy horses and they inspired me to play farmyards (not *Animal Farm* style) with their lead equivalents, and other animals, farmers and workers. Who knows, it may have sown the seeds of my wish in later life to organise people and events.

When we were not making our own fun and games in those and other ways there were times when Dad wasn't doing night shifts and we had special treats such as going to the Stratford Empire to see performers like Nellie Wallace, Elsie and Doris Walters, Max Miller, Teddy Brown, and Wilson, Keppel and Betty; or walking the length of the sewer to Woolwich to watch the pleasure boats going to and from Southend; and crossing the Thames on the Woolwich free ferry. Even more special were our trips to the London Palladium to see Peter Pan, and then graduating to the Crazy Gang.

With such ingredients our childhood in West Ham was varied and enjoyable but it was affected by the shift work Dad had to do throughout all the time we were growing up. His shifts were from 6-2, 2-10 and 10-6, which meant that he could only spend time with us in the 6-2 weeks, and even then there were times when he needed to rest. As a consequence it was left to Mum to organise and lead us in our out of school activities, a task which most parents usually share. The cinema trips, museum visits, shopping expeditions and participation in church activities were down to her.

The main activity I shared with Dad was going to West Ham home games, not every Saturday but most; but because going was usually a last minute decision due to Dad's tiredness, we never got to the ground in time to see the kick-off. But what Dad never failed to do was to take me after the match to Green Street market to get a bag of fruit to take to his brother, Uncle Len, and his family, who were more hard up than us.

Dad and I used to fish together from the promenade when we went on our holidays, first to Margate and then, going a bit more up-market, to Walton-on-the-Naze. We had one real treat for those holidays – being taken in Mr Burgess's car. He was a friend of the Newtons, the family who had a bicycle shop round the corner from us, and for whom I used to deliver accumulators for pocket money. I did that instead of my milk round: it paid a bit more (3s 6d a week) but the acid from the accumulators was tough on my trousers, and riding the converted ice-cream tricycle with its load was hard going. But it did give me my first sight of other people's homes in the East End, a revelation in itself. What did remain something of a mystery, however, was what other families did when they went "hopping" in Kent. They would go off in lorries filled up with their bedding and chairs and their pots and pans, but I always wondered what they did when they got there.

Less of a mystery was what one might call the "Lady Bountiful" moments when well-meaning better-off people sought to do charitable things for us, the less well-off inhabitants of the East End.

In our case, we had visits from Miss Knowles (who wrote novels under the name May Wynne) who also took us to tea at Lyons Corner House and introduced us to someone who worked at the BBC, while through our boys' club we were treated to a trip to a splendid country house at Westerham in Kent, where we met a wealthy racing driver, Jock Leith, and his friends. That was quite a contrast to the "ragged children" trip when we went by steam train (for the first time) all the way to Loughton in Essex, and spent the day catching tiddlers. But for most of us the best treat was being able to play indoor football in the hall of the Mission Church with coaching by a one-time professional footballer. One night at the boys' club I was allowed to do some sparring with a professional boxer, Nipper Fred Morris, who later married my cousin Rosie and invested in a hairdressing business in Dagenham, much used by the Ford workers.

Although my relations with Dad were always warm and friendly, I never discussed politics with him. This would have been due partly to his shift work but mainly, I think, because he was not particularly interested in politics or, so far as I could tell, union activity. Mum did express interest in some political issues and when I became the Labour candidate for Wallasey she joined the Party and became active in the women's section, and continued in it for some years. However, I did discuss politics with her brother, my uncle Arthur. He worked at Ciment Fondu, a cement plant at West Thurrock in Essex. He had strong left-wing views and told me about *The Ragged Trousered Philanthropists* and the activities of Sir Richard Acland and his Common Wealth movement. Although we did not always agree on issues, he was always ready to offer advice. So it was not surprising that many years later my old head teacher from West Ham, Dr Priestley, should tell the *Observer:* "Even at the age of 11 Fred was fascinated by politics."

Uncle Arthur was decidedly on the working-class wing of the Jones family, whereas Mum's sister, Daisy, had married into the middle class and lived in what to us was a "posh" house in Upminster that had a grandfather clock and always smelled strongly of furniture polish. Her husband, Frank, managed a shipping office in the City. He was very likeable; we did not discuss politics but we had a common loyalty to the Hammers since he was a season-ticket holder. His sons were the only members of our two families who went to university, until I became a student. Another of my mother's brothers was in the navy and became an officer on a warship, a painting of which held pride of place in my parents' bedroom. Her third brother was also in the navy, but he had married a Catholic and they seemed to be frozen out. Mum's fourth brother, Ted, had had meningitis as a child and had long spells out of work, endlessly searching for jobs. His passion was doing crosswords and *Tit-Bits* was his bible. I guess he was the intellectual of the Jones family, but caring for him became quite a burden for Mum.

There were, of course, family gatherings (though not after the Blitz had led to some of our relatives leaving West Ham) but I don't recall any time when both Dad's and Mum's relatives came together.

I never met any of our grandparents and never learned anything about my parents' childhood and upbringing. They never said what kind of school they had attended or what kind of work they had done, though I gleaned from family photos that Mum had worked in some kind of factory and Dad had been in the army before he came to work as a screensman in Vernon's flour mill (though I had no idea what that entailed). Dad's family all came from West Ham and they used to come to the parties held downstairs in our front room, complete with its aspidistra and gramophone. As they gossiped and joked over their port and lemon I tried to listen from the top of the stairs, in a manner reminiscent of Proust's description in *Remembrance of Times Past.*

Those family parties were jolly occasions, even when observed from the wings, but my happiest times in West Ham were those spent as a pupil at Plaistow Secondary School ("Plaistow Sec" as we called it). It was a great school and I can still put a name and face to all my teachers there, which is more than I can say of the elementary school I went to first and the grammar school in Wallasey where I finished my schooling after our move from West Ham. At Russell Road Elementary School I adored my first teacher, Miss Henry, and, like all the other pupils, lived in awe, if not fear, of the head, Mr Harding, who had a military bearing and a twirled, waxed moustache which made him look like Adolphe Menjou, the French officer in that great war film *Paths of Glory.* Those two apart, the only other teacher at the school who made an impression was the one who threw pieces of chalk at any pupil who misbehaved. I did, however, have one hero in the school, an older boy named Con Mahoney. He got a job as a messenger boy at the BBC and did well later, and he sent me signed photographs of BBC personalities like Henry Hall, Harry S. Pepper and Doris Arnold.

Plaistow Sec was something else. It was one of the only two selective schools in the borough, which had 250,000 inhabitants before the war reduced the population by half, and I always wondered why more of my fellow pupils at Russell Road were not allowed to go there. While I was at the school we were evacuated twice. The first time was to Weymouth when the war began (by mistake we were taken to Wellington in Somerset and transferred after a week). The second evacuation was to Newquay following the Blitz, in September 1940 (many pupils had returned to West Ham by the summer when no bombing had occurred). It was a measure of the quality of the staff that in spite of all the problems and pressures and upheavals that evacuation caused (including having to hold some classes in shops and church halls – rather like some of today's "free schools") our teachers managed to keep up morale and maintain the high standard of education the school provided and which HMI reports confirmed. They also kept up most of the extra-curricular activities which had made Plaistow Sec such a special place. Activities like teaching us ballroom dancing and running Friday night "hops", staging plays and Christmas shows (most notably the one in which the head played Hitler and the art master Mussolini, in devastating fashion), forming an orchestra and providing gramophone recitals, which gave the school its distinctive character, which was also reflected in its architecture – instead of the traditional three-decker it was single storey with the classrooms round two quadrangles.

While we were at Weymouth I edited and circulated a clandestine news-sheet entitled *The Martyr's Own.* It was not aimed at the teachers, but the way some of the "foster parents" were treating some of us evacuees. When the head attacked the news-sheet in assembly we changed the title to *Invicta* and carried on publishing, catering for the increased interest the head had stimulated by including the work of a star cartoonist.

Sadly, there was one aspect of the life of the school which, again, was no reflection on the staff and the quality of the education they provided but which had real social significance – the extent to which a substantial number of pupils left school before the age of 16 even though it was a selective school and performing well. During my time at the school only a handful of pupils stayed on in order to go to higher education. The seriousness of this situation was commented on by the head, Dr Priestley, and it continued in the immediate post-war years. He wrote: "In the first of these years (1945-48) more than a third of the pupils left before the age of 16, in the second more than two-fifths, and in the third, more than half. That such premature withdrawal is largely due to economic reasons no one will deny. The proportion of really able boys and girls who leave, often without a school certificate, is disappointingly high." I emphasise this in view of the attempts made nowadays by right-wing politicians and commentators who have tried to rubbish the achievements of post-war governments, Conservative as well as Labour, by talking of the "dumbing down" in education which they say has been caused by the introduction of comprehensive education and the decline of the grammar schools.

Happily the buildings of Plaistow Sec survived the bombing of the East End and today they are the site of NewVIc – the biggest sixth form college in London which, while still serving the same less-than-affluent part of London, is enabling many hundreds of students to go on to higher and further education. The contrast with what happened in my time could not be more stark.

In due course I myself became one of those who did not stay on at school to benefit from further study. When our family had to move to Wallasey due to my father's transfer to another flour mill, my brother and I were transferred to Oldershaw Grammar School. I suppose I was not there long enough to become as attached to the school as I was to Plaistow Sec but I felt it was an altogether less dynamic place (and it was not a mixed school), although I did make some good friendships there, including one with Josephine, the head girl of the adjacent girls' grammar school, which lasted until I joined the army. The head of Oldershaw wanted me to stay on into the sixth form but my parents could not afford that and I left at the age of 16, an experience that convinced me of the value of the education maintenance allowance which, to its credit, Labour introduced after the 1997 election.

Although I had to leave school very reluctantly, my education on a broader basis, and especially in politics and social affairs, was to continue by other means, as I shall explain later.

Progressive youth

"Politics ran through the streets. Even at the age of 11, Fred was fascinated by them."
– Harold Priestley, Fred's headmaster in West Ham

Thanks to the war-time truce between the main parties, there was virtually no political activity in Wallasey when we arrived there from West Ham in 1941. Not that there would have been much anyway. It was, at that time, a rock-solid Tory seat represented at Westminster by Lt-Col John Moore-Brabazon. He later became notorious and was forced to resign from the Government when he expressed the hope that Germany and the Soviet Union (Britain's ally in the war) would destroy each other.

There were, however, two organisations showing signs of life, both in effect and origin Communist Party front outfits. They were the Progressive Youth Movement (PYM) and the Socialist Discussion Group. The PYM was the more interesting because it had no adult leaders. Its membership was drawn largely from pupils and ex-pupils of the town's three grammar schools and it had an ambitious programme of talks and debates, theatre trips and rambles as well as discussing political issues. Among the speakers we had were Olaf Stapledon, the philosopher, "Ralph", a veteran of the Spanish Civil War and Les Parrington who told us of the monstrosities of apartheid in South Africa. We also heard Dr Lennox Johnstone, an outspoken and dedicated medic who even in those days exposed the link between smoking and cancer, a man clearly well ahead of his time. I heard of the PYM just before I left school and soon joined, there being no other body catering for my growing interest in politics. At that time the leading light in the PYM was a young Communist, Ted Bedford, who was to become the party's rising star on Merseyside. In due course he went to London where he became secretary of the London Co-operative Party, a career which, sadly for him, came to an end when he was accused of embezzlement.

Whatever expectations the CP might have had of using the PYM for its own ends evaporated as the membership grew and broadened. I became editor of its magazine *Youth Forward* and wrote reports of our meetings for the *Wallasey News* and the *Liverpool Echo* and *Evening Express* which paid me the princely sum of a penny-halfpenny a line for my copy. I sent the magazine to Harold Dent, the great editor of the *Times Educational Supplement,* John Wolfenden, at that time headmaster of Uppingham, and Honor Balfour, broadcaster and then London editor of Time magazine. They all sent very supportive letters and from that I developed a long friendship with Harold who published my first serious article for the *TES* while I was in the army. Honor was to become Common Wealth candidate in the Darwen by-election and I went and spent time with her in the constituency while in barracks at Bamber Bridges, Preston. I met John Wolfenden again after the war when he was vice-chancellor of Reading University and my wife-to-be, Anne, held a research fellowship there.

One of the outcomes of our activities in PYM was to secure a place on the borough's youth committee and I became its representative. It was quite a lark when, before my first meeting, the councillors were taking tea and my boss, H.R.B. Wood, the director of education, walked in to find me, his most junior clerk, sitting and chatting with them.

The CP had a bit more of a grip on the Socialist Discussion Group, but in spite of that I became secretary of the group and before I joined the army I organised two big public meetings for it. The first, to urge medical aid to Russia (after it had been invaded by Hitler's armies), was memorable for a superb speech by Sidney Silverman, the diminutive MP for Nelson and Colne. Later I organised a meeting calling for independence for India. That one was memorable for me because I spent time afterwards chatting with the speaker, Krishna Menon, who became the first Indian High Commissioner in London after independence.

Somewhat more turbulent was the occasion when I had invited a leading Merseyside Trotskyite to address the group. Not surprisingly, his remarks sent some members up the wall, but they gave me an early insight into relationships, or rather the lack of them, between the Stalinists and the Trotskyites and so was helpful to the political education of an

18-year old (though not so relevant to my service in the Home Guard, and my fire-watching at the public library, that were my other main spare time activities).

One tremor disturbed the political tranquility of war-time Wallasey and that arose from the 1943 by-election. Lt-Col Moore-Brabazon had been forced to resign his seat following his injudicious remarks about the Soviet Union and although Labour and the Liberals observed the truce, a maverick former Labour councillor, George Reakes, did not. He challenged the widely respected Tory councillor, John Pennington, and won. Great shock all round.

While the Socialist Discussion Group did not survive the war, the PYM did. With the return of members from war service it changed its name to the Wallasey Progressive Movement and added to its activities a number of "revues" enlivened by the wit of my friend Art Selling, and in which I did a Groucho Marx routine (based on his gags written down at the cinema). It also led to the creation of the Wallasey Jazz Club which, in turn, led to the birth of the Merseysippi Jazz Band. The driving force behind the band was Dick Goodwin, who worked alongside me at the education department at Wallasey town hall. It was great to follow the success of the band – they played gigs in London and the US and went on to play at the Cavern in Liverpool where the Beatles were to play during the intervals in the band's performances.

I gave up editorship of the WPM magazine because of the growing demands on my time made by running the Labour Society at Liverpool University and by my membership of the national executive of the NUS. The new editor of the magazine was my girlfriend, a young teacher named Hazel Jones. I thought that relationship was flourishing (we had been on a trip to Paris together, after all) until, some two months before my final exams, she told me that she had found someone else. This arose from her taking part in, of all things, a production at the WPM of Sartre's *Huis Clos* together with one Clive Fell. Sad though that news was, it did have a silver lining. My response was, as they put it, to throw myself into my academic work to which, up to that point, I had hardly been 100% committed. I guess it paid off: when the exam results were announced, to my great surprise I had been awarded the Social Science Certificate with Distinction. All in all, therefore, I had a lot to be thankful for as a result of my experiences in the PYM, WPM and Socialist Discussion Group and from the many friendships I made in them, and especially with Hazel, with whom I kept in touch for many years until she and Clive tragically were killed in a car crash.

With my various activities in Wallasey, and with the Youth Parliament we founded after the war, I had become fairly well known in the borough, notwithstanding my cockney origins. I had joined the Labour Party after demobilisation and began to attend its meetings, became a ward chairman, in addition to my work in the university Labour Society and my chairmanship of the Labour Party's national student organisation (NALSO). In the 1945 general election Labour decided to fight the Wallasey seat, though in my opinion it would have been wiser not to challenge George Reakes in the hope that his re-election would break the traditional Tory hold on the seat. The result was a Tory winning on a minority of the votes.

When it came to the 1951 general election I was asked to stand as the Labour candidate. I had become deputy president of the NUS and, having finished my studies, was starting a year's research studentship at Oxford delegacy for social studies (Barnett House) but I still felt I could accept the nomination.

Making hay at the Hay Festival –
and remembering my 'gap years'

One of the pleasures in attending the Hay Festival is the opportunity it provides, if one is lucky, to put questions to the distinguished (and less distinguished) authors who have come to promote their latest books and talk about life in general.

One year among the authors on parade (although I'm not sure he had actually written a book) was John Boulton, the arch-neo-liberal interventionist from the USA. Boulton regularly performed on our TV screens until even the Bush administration had had enough of him. Prior to his appearance at the festival, George Monbiot of the *Guardian* had announced his intention to effect a "citizen's arrest" of Boulton on the spot. Surrounded by friends in the audience, Monbiot was clearly intent on the brave deed; however, when I spotted a couple of heavies at the front of the stage I thought "you'll be lucky mate" and, of course, Monbiot got nowhere near his quarry.

That left the way open for questions to Boulton and I got in early. First I asked: "When you lost your post as US Ambassador to the UN, did you jump or were you pushed?", and second: "Given that your policy as an interventionist is to assert that the US is entitled to take pre-emptive action against other states if it feels its interests are threatened, are you prepared to allow Russia and China the same right?" Boulton laughed and in reply to the first question said "I resigned." He did not answer the second question.

I had a more heated encounter a year later at Hay with Anthony Beevor, an author whose books I have admired. He had come to talk about his latest book, *D-Day: the Battle for Normandy,* which, like his books on Stalingrad and the fall of Berlin, was a graphic and well-researched account of a major episode in the Second World War. When it came to questions I said to Beevor: "When you launched your book you were reported in the press as saying that the bombardment of Caen was tantamount to a war crime. I took part in that bombardment along with a lot of my compatriots over a period of weeks. At no time did I feel that I was guilty of a war crime – should I have done?" The applause from the audience doubtless made Beevor feel more angry than he felt already about my remarks and he replied that his words had been misrepresented in the press and that he had been referring to the aerial bombardment of Caen and not the shelling by our troops.

That exchange was more dramatic than virtually anything that happened to me in the course of my army career, with the possible exception of two encounters with irate sergeant majors. The first of those occurred while I was in training in Scarborough and learning to ride a motor bike (not one of my favourite occupations). I was having difficulty in kick-starting the bike and suddenly felt warmth between my legs. A spark had ignited petrol that had splashed on to the tank. I was about to discover that sergeant majors tend not to be the most soft spoken of men as ours rushed up, furious and wielding a fire extinguisher as he called me all the names under the sun, and put the fire out in the nick of time. Talk about occupying the hot seat!

The second colourful bollocking came from another sergeant major not long after we had arrived in Normandy on D+4. In embarking from the landing craft we had to wade ashore with water up to our chests and holding our rifles above our heads. Soaked to the skin we marched inland and, with the sun coming up, halted and took off as much clothing as we dared to dry off. What seemed to us a sensible step brought down the wrath of the sergeant major who yelled that our white under-clothes were presenting a target to enemy aircraft (or words to that effect) and the sooner we got fully dressed, the better.

Apart from those two colourful verbal assaults, I guess I had what might be called a "quiet" war by comparison with the dangers and horrors suffered by many of our troops on D-Day and thereafter, and on many other war fronts. Indeed, I came nearer to real danger during the bombing in West Ham and Wallasey than in France, Belgium, Holland and Germany. After landing in Normandy there were a few occasions when enemy shells fell relatively near but for the most part the gunfire to which I became accustomed was that from the 25-pounder guns of the battery to which I was sent as a signaller and with which I remained until hostilities ended.

There were, of course, experiences one would never have had but for the years in the army and I wrote about some of them in my Forces Diary, which appeared regularly in the *Wallasey News* for most of my active service. My purpose in writing the column had been to give readers some idea of the day-to-day life of at least some of those whose "gap years" were spent in pursuits wholly different from those of the post-war generations, as I hope these extracts from my diary will indicate.

France, September 1944

Victory, when it comes, will bring many great problems in Europe which we in Europe and the US will be unable to ignore, for it will be to us that the liberated people will look for salvation. Every day out here makes me realise more and more the colossal nature of one of these problems (and as yet I can know only how it affects France) – housing.

As the war swept across her plains, it left behind in France a trail of shattered homes. Just now one does not notice the result of this so much because where homes are destroyed the people are gone, and no problem of homeless people seems to exist. The answer is that the families whose homes are now rubble, if they are not dead, are to be found sleeping in barns on farms, and in the houses of more fortunate friends. They have left their native towns and villages as the tide of battle approached, carrying with them only a suit-case and, if they were lucky and had a cart, some bedding, but very little else. To all intents and purposes they have nothing. In summer they can bear with the shabby little life which these conditions impose, but when winter comes things will be different. These refugees will need real shelter, they will need food, and they will need clothing. One can understand their anxiety, expressed by the woman who asked, "When will the houses promised by the Americans arrive?"

To the virtually helpless refugees of St Lo and Sourdeval, Caen and Caumont, and many other ravaged towns and villages, this housing problem is a very, very urgent one. Do people in Britain and distant America see it in the same light?

I fancy most of our cartoonists and a few people besides would have been a trifle disappointed by a bunch of German prisoners I recently chanced to observe more closely than had previously been my fortune. A motley crew, they were earning their keep doing cook-house fatigues. Ranging from mere boys of 14 or so, to middle-aged and scraggy men, they were for the most part wretched; pride was the last thing they possessed. The trouble was, look though I may, I could find no square heads and their uniforms were dishevelled; but what prisoners of war aren't like that? Take them out of their grey-green (it's a rotten colour anyway), fling their jack-boots, wash and shave them, put them in khaki and who knows, even our cartoonists couldn't say they wouldn't look British.

Belgium, October 1944

I suppose it was most unromantic of me to be asleep at the time when our truck crossed the border into Belgium, for at one time (I do not know if it persists) such occasions were regarded by "foreigners" as a thing of import, a subject for sentimentality. Apparently the crossing of a line from one country into another called for a deep inhaling of breath on the soil of the country one was about to leave and, with the first exhalation on the new land, the words "So this is —."

My own experience only served to show how lacking in realism all that is, and to make me ask again about frontiers and their future. Are they not signs of a past age, the hangover from days of petty nationalisms which did their best to bring about wars? Can countries be made really separate and complete entities by the drawing of lines across maps? Is it too much to hope that in a saner future men will show wisdom by forming Federations of states, wherein frontiers serve much the same purpose as our county boundaries, but nothing more?

It was dark when I was asleep in France; light had been with the world at least three hours before I awoke. Yet had I not been told, there was little to show I had left France. The people looked the same, most of them spoke the same language – though with a different dialect, the road signs were unchanged, and the children awaiting the passing trucks with outstretched hands still cried "Ceegarette pour papa." There was, I agree, a more urban appearance about the more frequently occurring towns, resulting from the greater degree of industrialisation which Belgium enjoys (?), but I am convinced that there was no outstanding difference to drawing a line between the two countries, labelling them so distinctly the one FRANCE and the other BELGIUM, and thinking they are thus made separate and sovereign. They are not; they are of one world, as indeed all Europe is.

Holland, December 1944

It is raining outside; it seems to have done nothing else for the past week; and there seems to be no prospect of it doing anything else for at least another week. I sit here in damp clothes, the steam rising from my drying hands, from my coat, my boots and my hat. From outside there comes the distant drone of many aeroplanes, out again to bomb Germany and astounding us by their apparent disregard of the weather; a truck groans as it lurches through the oozing, deceiving weals of mud on an errand.

The time for evening meal approaches and with it, darkness, making the view from here even more dreary. What I see now holds nothing of that Holland I once saw in paint and story books; there are no clogs, no white aprons, half-moon hats, tulips or windmills. My panorama is just one solitary, scraggy sand-dune, sparely adorned with tufts of comfortless needle-like shrub and shell-holes, which so spreads its ugly self as to leave room for nothing but the low, grey, rain-laden clouds whisking speedily on their way above it; and on either side there is more sand, more of that miserable sticky stuff which seeps into mess-tins and food, clings to wet clothes, gradually silts up hair, and finds its way – there is no privacy – yes, even into bed and blankets.

It is not without thankfulness, therefore, that one turns from this desolate exterior to the refuge of the ramshackle bivouac. Although it is not the best of places one would choose – even a hermit might refuse it – in times like these one is grateful for what little comfort it brings. A hole dug while rains came, some duckboards from the place that was a brickworks, a plank or two, and a motley array of covers – these are the ingredients which in the course of a few hours became a "home". A home in which the occupants do everything at the kneel for fear of knocking their heads on the already shaky roof. Where blankets are heaped in orderly confusion by day and at night, if only for a few hours, become beds wherein sleepers lie tightly packed, their length sandwiched between two sandy walls. Maybe it leaks a little when one of the pools which always seems to collect on the sloping roof is disturbed; maybe the gas cape draped across that awkward hole (which is cursed regularly at every entrance and exit) called the door, doesn't keep out all the wind and rain it should, and perhaps those holes over on that side there could be blocked up with something; maybe it could have been better protected from those shells the "Boche" finds time to lob over – in spite of everything, it always looks much too big. Maybe all those things, and a few more beside, but one is still glad of it in times like these.

Germany, April 1945

The end is not far off now, or so they tell me. Once the final onslaught over the Rhine has been made and the drive for the heart of the Reich begun, it won't last much longer than a month, at least that's what our battery commander reckons, and according to him he's not generally an optimist. At any rate, it will not be many weeks now before the German Army capitulates and the Third Reich disintegrates into a terrible chaos.

A preview of what that chaos will be like has been afforded us by what we have seen in the past few weeks of the small portion of Germany at present in allied hands. I have seen Goch and one or two other towns of size; they are completely shattered and to all intents and purposes, citizenless. I do not doubt that the same can be said of every other German town captured so far by the Second Army.

In their houses, evidence of Nazism is not lacking. Whilst most families have taken the trouble to remove any evidence of membership of Nazi organisations, they haven't bothered or had time to destroy books, papers, or photos of the National Socialist leaders, their disreputable achievements, Nazi rallies, *Wehrmacht* parades, etc. This, I suppose, is because such things were more or less obligatory ornaments and not necessarily a sign of one's feelings towards the Nazis. Equally, or even more prominent than the signs of Hitler's regime, are the signs of that of the Pope. In not one house I have entered have I failed to find the usual manifestations of Roman Catholicism. Crucifixes, rosaries, religious tracts and pictures, all are to be found in large numbers. That they should exist alongside the material of Nazism and snaps of smiling sons and daughters in the *Wehrmacht, Luftwaffe, Hitler Jugend, SS,* etc, is something which will make the inquisitive person more inquisitive.

Although I reserve full judgment until I have been into more homes of the poorer classes, it does appear that German families have gone short of very little in this war. Most cellars are well stored with preserved fruit and vegetables; whilst the farms have plenty of livestock and fowl. Furniture and clothing, though possibly *ersatz,* is invariably bright, modernistic and plentiful. And coalless people in England might care to know that few Germans have been as badly off as (a good many have been much better off than) themselves. But one has no doubts whatsoever that the same will not be true of German households from now on. The future for them is black indeed.

Germany, June 1945

Germany's Armies are defeated and the liberation of the people they had oppressed has, at least technically, been achieved. There remains now the hardly less important task of re-settling Europe's scattered millions and reconstructing her shattered lands, and of governing Germany until the time comes when the Germans themselves show their ability and willingness to establish a Government strong enough to rule decently and purge Germany of all taint of Nazism.

A major part in that great task will be played by the Allied Armies of Occupation; it has already been commenced. The transition from action to occupation was quite smooth for our Regiment, and we are already acclimatised to living relatively normal lives once more. (How frightful it is to have to wash every morning before breakfast in proper basins; to have to eat at a table, sleep on a bed, and parade like recruits; to have to polish brasses, blanco, maintain over-maintained equipment, etc, etc. As somebody said: "It's just like being in the peace-time army, only more so.")

After coming out of action – we eventually ended up on the outskirts of Bremen but celebrated VE very anticlimactically in as peaceful a spot as one could hope to find, a village set beautifully 'midst the hills near Osnabruck – we kicked off with a Garrison job guarding, curfew patrolling, werewolf hunting. Lately we have been guarding Displaced Persons and ex-POW camps.

Just now there are millions of DPs and ex-POWs in Germany, all wanting to go home. It is the nerve-testing job of British, American and, I presume, Russian officers and men, to tell those millions that, unfortunately, they cannot go home; at least, not yet awhile. And in the meantime they have to be made as comfortable as possible.

If the active service part of my army days was relatively quiet, the remainder of my time in khaki verged on the "cushy". But it was not only cushy; it was also a slice of luck that had a profound effect on my future.

When hostilities ended in Europe our battery was shelling Bremen and for a short spell we were assigned to guarding prisoners of war prior to transfer to other duties. When the transfers came through, my mate Jack Jameson was to be sent to Burma while I was to return to London for training in preparation for transfer to military government. We were dismayed, for Jack and I had been together throughout our training and the invasion and its aftermath. I don't know how those postings were decided but if it had been based simply on an alphabetical order on a list and the line drawn differently I could well have been sent to Burma, where the war was continuing, my health could have been undermined, as Jack's was, and I would never have had the life-changing opportunity that the posting to military government provided. As they say, you never know your luck. I certainly appreciated mine.

The military government unit that I joined was based on the north-western tip of Schleswig-Holstein and included the islands of Föhr, Amrun and Sylt, a popular German holiday resort. It had suffered little war damage, unlike the nearby port of Kiel, and adjoined the Danish frontier. It was administered from the town hall of the county town of Niebull and we lived in an architect's house. Our transport included a Mercedes Benz, a Buick and a Harley Davidson (heaven knows how they got to Niebull) and a launch to take us to the islands. I was promoted to the rank of sergeant when I took charge of the office and with official approval I also began the organisation of a number of youth groups run on similar lines to the Progressive Youth Movement we had in Wallasey. I developed that work in conjunction with the Earl of Buckinghamshire, who was the officer in charge at Kiel HQ.

With the onset of "fraternisation" I greatly enjoyed the friendship (but not simultaneously) of three very attractive *frauleins* – Gerti, Uschi and Effie – but not to the extent that they might hamper what was to be my life-changing experience. Having left school at 16, I realised I needed to get some further education if I was to have any hope of a career so I asked Ruskin College for help. They readily agreed and I began a correspondence course with the college. Conditions in Niebull were such that I could do the reading and essays without difficulty. I also had the benefit of a spell at Gottingen University through an army education scheme (while there I met John Mendelsohn who later became a Labour MP). The result of my studies was that I entered for and was awarded a Jack Lawson scholarship at Ruskin and was due to take it up on demobilisation.

There have been times over recent years as student loans have been introduced when I have had a sense of guilt that today's students have been denied the free higher education that we ex-service men and women received through FETS, the Further Education and Training Scheme. But then I reflect that, unlike today's students, our years in the services truly were "gap" years, years in which normal life and choices were taken away from us, whether we liked it or not.

Student days

Shirley Williams remembers him as "a man among boys".

"Already he had a natural feel for politics at a time when most of his fellows were still wet behind the ears. He was a very sophisticated figure."

With the award of a Jack Lawson scholarship I was expecting to go to Ruskin College after demobilisation but I also received a suggestion of an alternative possibility from a friend in Wallasey, Norman Wilson, son of the editor of the *Wallasey News*. He was a lecturer at Liverpool University's social science department and said its social science certificate course was one of the best in the country. He suggested I should consider applying for it. He knew I did not have a higher school certificate and so could not take a degree course but felt I would be accepted for the certificate course. So I applied for a place with the hope that I would take up the Ruskin scholarship afterward. Ruskin agreed I could do that, so I went to Liverpool in September 1947. Norman was right about the course – it was excellent and I greatly enjoyed it.

When I started at Liverpool I discovered there was no Labour Society in the student union. There was the Socialist Society but it was affiliated to the fellow-travelling Student Labour Federation, so I got together with some Labour supporters and set up a Labour Society. We affiliated to NALSO, Labour's national student organisation, and I went as a delegate to its national conference. Having already been sent as a Liverpool delegate to the council of the National Union of Students, I criticised the NALSO leadership for the association's failure to take an effective part in the life of the NUS. This led to my election to the NALSO executive, with responsibility for NUS matters.

Thus I had become involved in the work of both the NUS and NALSO within weeks of becoming a student and they became my chief preoccupation from that point on – though I did try to find time for studying, and my girlfriend Hazel and the Wallasey Progressive Movement too.

One enjoyable interlude in my Liverpool course was my vacation activity. In my first summer vacation I spent time in the Midlands town of Dudley taking part in a social survey being carried out by the social services department (and watching cricket for the first and almost only time in my life). Much more exciting was attending a summer course at Zurich University the following year. A friend in the Liverpool department, Ron Gass, told me of the course which was being run under the direction of an American academic – one Dr Henry Kissinger. Needless to say, that was in his earlier days, but it would still have been interesting to meet him. That didn't happen, but I did meet Kingsley Martin, the editor of the *New Statesman,* who was lecturing at the course. I was a keen reader of the *Statesman,* and Martin's weekly London Diary had given me the idea for the Forces Diary which I wrote for the *Wallasey News* when I was in the army. So it was great to meet him, and I interviewed him for the WPM magazine. The other major personality I met while in Zurich was the great Swiss theologian, Dr Karl Barth. A group of us from the summer school were invited to his house for a meal and discussion. It was a fascinating experience, the most bizarre aspect of which was that his wife was present but took no part whatsoever in the whole proceedings. After our studies at Liverpool, Ron Gass and I met again in Oxford before he went on to become the first sociologist to join the civil service. Many years later we were to meet again in Paris, where Ron had become head of education and human resources at the OECD and I was taking part as a union representative.

If it is said that you should start off as you mean to continue, I guess that's what happened to me in those days. As I've already explained (Progressive Youth), what did change was that my girlfriend ended our relationship about two months before my final exams and as a result I threw myself into my academic work and, to my astonishment, was awarded a distinction in the social science certificate. I was then asked to see the head of the department, Professor T.S. Simey, who wanted to know what I intended to do next. I told him I would be taking up the scholarship at Ruskin but he said I should do a degree. I said that was all very well but (a) I had no higher school certificate and

(b) Oxford would already be full up with ex-service applicants. He said, "Leave it to me"! A few days later I was invited to an interview with Professor Asa Briggs in Oxford. He was acting on behalf of a delegacy for (I think) mature students. As luck would have it (again), somebody dropped out at the last minute at St Catherine's Society and I was given his place. What was bizarre about the whole business (though very pleasing too) was that whereas I was not able to take a degree course at Liverpool University I was able to do so at Oxford.

So I gave up the Ruskin scholarship and started a shortened honours course in politics, philosophy and economics. I had a great time, with Wilfred Knapp and D.N. Chester (who became head of Nuffield College) among my tutors and only one blip along the way.

My first tutor, Dr Duncan, was blind, and I suppose as a consequence was not familiar with all the minutiae of Oxford's course regulations. Unwittingly, when I selected the six subjects I intended to study one of them did not meet the regulator's requirements. This was only discovered when I went to the examination schools to enter for the final exams. I was then told that I had to offer another subject – with only weeks to go. I told Wilfred Knapp the disastrous news but he said he would seek a special dispensation to enable me to take the "wrong" subject. Meanwhile I'd better start studying the "right" one! It was a massive relief when Wilfred told me a fortnight later that the special dispensation had been agreed. So I was able to get on with revising.

That upset apart, I got a great deal from my tutorials and some great lectures, especially those of Tony Crosland and K.C. Whear, and from the immense variety of events put on by the clubs and societies, or rather from as many as I could fit in given the time I had to give to the NUS and NALSO. I had become deputy president of NUS and chairman of NALSO, and the commitments they involved led the writer of my "Isis Idol" to describe me as "perhaps the busiest man in Oxford". It also led my tutor Wilfred Knapp to say, when telling me of my exam results, that he hoped I would be happy with my 2:1, adding: "I suppose you would have been pleased with a first but I suppose you can't run the Labour Party and take a first as well."

After I had finished my PPE course I was awarded a research studentship at the delegacy for social studies (Barnett House). I set out to explore the differences between statutory social services and voluntary agencies, and what was said to be the inflexibility of the former and the flexibility of the latter. Although I did all the fieldwork I had planned (and all the tutoring I had to give), by the time it came to writing up the results I was under great pressure at the NUS and then from the 1951 general election, for which I had been selected as the Labour candidate for Wallasey. To my great regret, and in spite of my hopes of returning to it, I was not able to complete the work. Not surprisingly, the delegacy said that it would not feel able to commend me further if I did not deliver. Who could blame them?

The electors of Wallasey didn't deliver either. We had a lively campaign with big meetings – one, which was packed, addressed by that great character Bessie Braddock – and others where I used new techniques and had support from Alf Morris and fellow students from Jamaica and Trinidad. However, although I achieved the biggest swing to Labour on Merseyside in the election, and notwithstanding the eve of poll view of my agent, Bill Clements, that we were "in with a chance" (moral: never trust your agent), I lost to Ernest Marples by over 15,000 votes and Wallasey continued on the Conservative path – but not forever. It has now been Labour (as part of the Wirral constituency) for more than 20 years and has an excellent MP in Angela Eagle. While my academic career had come to an end, my new role as president of the NUS was soon to begin.

On the Oxford scene itself I wrote a number of articles for *Isis,* the excellent and principal Oxford publication in those days. In one article I crossed swords with William Rees-Mogg, a president of the Oxford Union and later to become editor of *The Times* and a member of the House of Lords. In an exchange of views about the differences between the Conservative and Labour Parties, I said, among other things, the following:

> "For a quarter of a century," Rees-Mogg says, "the rich have been getting poorer and the standard of living of the most unfortunate has been steadily improving." One can almost see the paupers of Park Lane rubbing shoulders

with the nouveaux riches of Mile End! The truth is that in spite of the basic minimum which our social services now provide, millions of families are still spending less on a week's living than most of the upper income groups are able to spend on an evening's entertainment. Because of this, there are many people who believe that the "two nations" still exist and one reason for their support of the Labour Party is a desire to end such a state of affairs.

Are we to be divided from this circus only by a vague tiff over the use of power? I, for one, prefer to believe that the division still rests on a fundamental difference in outlook concerning the causes of, and remedies for the political, social and economic problems of our time. For me, the Conservatives remain what their actions have always showed them to be – the guardians of the rights of profit and the vast economic power of capitalism; the champions of selfish individual interests; and the party which believes it has a "divine right" to rule the people of Britain.

Mr Rees-Mogg's earnest talk about the "diffusion of power" cannot conceal these facts and will be recognised as the red herring it really is. It does not mean much to millions of Britons to picture the State as a big bogey man, reducing them all to serfdom. They see State action as a means of developing human personality, not of frustrating it.

But of course this new Conservative argument is clearly aimed at gaining the support of the Liberals. By using the vague phrases of Liberal doctrines, the Tories hope to persuade the Liberals that their party is carrying on the Liberal tradition. One hopes, however, that there are enough Liberals of the radical variety left in Oxford to see through this hollow manoeuvre and recognise which party is giving practical effect to their radicalism!

Although written more than 60 years ago, I feel those words have some relevance to what is happening in our country at the present time.

I attended the debates at the Oxford Union regularly but was not interested in seeking office there; I already had plenty on my plate with the NUS. I did, however, make one "paper" speech when I led the opposition to German re-armament. I managed to lose my notes before the debate began but pressed on, leading the Union president, Godfrey Smith, to make some very complimentary remarks about my speech in the *Oxford Magazine.*

I was certainly not alone in my disappointment and sadness over the result of the 1951 general election. For many of us in the Labour movement it was a profound shock too, given how much the Attlee government had achieved for our war-stricken country since 1945. But in addition to the shock, it left us with plenty of questions about what could have gone wrong and what should have been done but wasn't.

Realising that there were issues that we in the Labour Party's student organisation (NALSO) ought to discuss and help to develop, I proposed that we should organise a "Socialist Stocktaking School". That was long before the days of "think-tanks", and only the Fabian Society might have done something like it. The NALSO committee agreed to the idea so I then set about devising a framework for the school. To do that I sought the help of Professor G.D.H. Cole, then of All Souls College. These days he would, no doubt, be called a "guru" but in those days he had become the *éminence grise* of the Labour movement, thanks to his many and distinguished books and pamphlets, and lectures on key issues. At Oxford, Cole held court in his rooms at All Souls for what was known as the "Cole Group", and which was attended, by prized invitation, by dons and undergraduates. I was one who sat physically, but not philosophically, at Cole's feet, and questioned some of his assertions, but I could think of no-one better able to give advice on the issues our stocktaking school should consider, and possible speakers.

One of the issues I particularly felt needed discussion, especially in view of the experience of nationalisation, was industrial democracy. Cole agreed, but when I said I thought Herbert Morrison might be the person to deal with that issue he almost exploded, declaring that Morrison was the biggest enemy of industrial democracy in the country! So Herbert was out.

We held the school at Transport House and it was very well attended – Shirley Williams and Bill

Rogers were among my fellow Oxford students who participated – but we did not come up with many answers to the questions Labour would be facing. And it would soon be time for me to prepare myself for the issues and questions I would face when I took my position as president of the National Union of Students to which I had been elected.

Part 2: Into battle

Strength and struggle in the NUS

I need to declare an interest in respect of this chapter, inasmuch as the National Union of Students presented me with its first lifetime service award in 2009. That left me feeling even more warm and grateful to the union and, it might be thought by readers, less than objective about the organisation. But what follows is not a judgment on the worth and effectiveness of the union so much as an account of my experiences arising from my involvement in and association with it.

Today the National Union of Students is the biggest democratic and representative organisation of young men and women in Europe. With some seven million members of its affiliated student unions in England, Scotland, Wales and Northern Ireland it is even bigger than the total membership of the TUC's affiliated unions.

It has grown massively since its foundation in 1922, and is far bigger than it was when I first became involved as a delegate to its conference in 1947. In those days we counted the membership in tens of thousands; today they are counted in millions. This enormous growth reflects the great expansion of higher and further education which has occurred in the British Isles. The growth of the

NUS was not automatic, however. The individual student unions are free to affiliate (and disaffiliate) but while there have been some ups and downs and roller-coaster episodes at a number of points since the war, the union is now stronger financially and provides more services to its members than at any previous time in its 91 year history. Given the transitory nature of its membership – most students are on courses of three or four years' duration – the strength and stability, and growing influence, of the NUS is a tribute to the high quality of the elected leadership and the chief executive officer and large permanent staff of the union.

There was, however, a period when internal divisions threatened the very existence of the organisation. This came not long after I attended my first NUS conference (though, I hasten to add, it didn't arise from it). The cause of the serious division arose not from domestic issues like grants or fees, but the union's international relations. The members have always attached great importance to links with students in other countries, for its foundation was due to a wish for British students to take part in an international body that had been established after the First World War – the *Confédération Internationale des Etudiants* (CIE).

At the time there was no national body representing students in this country, and Ivison Macadam took the lead in establishing one so that this country's students could link with their counterparts abroad. The participation in the international body and the development of student travel were the main activities of the NUS until the outbreak of the Second World War.

In time, following disagreements on policy, the NUS disaffiliated from the CIE but continued with its travel and other activities, giving support to worthy causes and refugees, but on the outbreak of the Second World War its leadership followed the Communist Party line (in the wake of the Molotov-Ribbentrop pact) and got the NUS conference to condemn the war. This had serious internal repercussions but in due course the Communist Party line changed when Nazi Germany attacked the Soviet Union.

When the war ended, the NUS joined with other unions in establishing the International Union of Students (IUS), with its headquarters in Prague. The high hopes that the new organisation would play its part in restoring friendship and co-operation among the nations after the horrors of the war proved to be short lived. Not all the student unions in the democratic countries joined, and the Scottish Union of Students disaffiliated in 1946. Indications of the dangers of Communist domination and perversion of the organisation were not long in coming. Following the Communist coup in Czechoslovakia in 1948, the IUS leadership made no attempt to condemn the arrest of Czech student leaders, in spite of NUS protests. Even more blatant evidence of the IUS leadership's readiness to serve the Stalinist cause came when, after the rift between Stalin and Tito and the expulsion of Yugoslavia from the Cominform, the IUS leadership decided to expel the Yugoslav students' union and connived at the arrest of that union's representative at a meeting in Prague. Again the NUS leadership protested strongly, called for the readmission of the Yugoslavs and gave notice that it would pursue the issue at a meeting of the IUS executive which was to be held in London, and at the forthcoming IUS congress in Prague in August 1950. The IUS leadership completely rejected the protests and refused to readmit the Yugoslav union.

If those actions were bad enough, much worse was to follow from Prague. I wrote an account of what happened in the congress and I quote from it now because I want to suggest that what happened within the NUS following our return, while not quite as alarming, was almost as astounding as what took place at the congress. In my account I wrote:

The 850 delegates from 85 organisations representing 72 countries with a membership of 5,064,035 students went to Prague to dedicate themselves to the "fight for peace, national independence and a democratic education". Peace can take various forms, however, so it was necessary for Dr Nejedly, Czech minister of education, to indicate the sort of peace the IUS was seeking.

"We do not want any kind of peace," he told us; "we want a real peace which can only be brought about by socialism and communism. When we say 'Long live peace' we must also say 'Down with capitalism, down with imperialism; long live socialism, long live communism'."

There were times, however, when even peace took second place to the war of "liberation" in Korea, in the proceedings of the congress. The Korean (not north, not south, just Korean) delegation included one Lt-Col Kan Buk and a Lt Kim Pe-Chyn, who were given a place of honour. And just to show that IUS puts first things first the meeting obliged by passing a resolution crying "Death to the American invaders of Korea"; the first big demonstration, lasting nearly half an hour, was for Korea; and in the awarding of "peace flags" the largest went to the Korean delegation.

Indeed, the only delegation to receive equal attention was that of the British NUS. Many speakers made reference to us in their speeches from the rostrum, the name of Mr Stanley Jenkins, president of the NUS, being mentioned nearly 200 times, whilst "the leaders" were frequently referred to as "servants of the Anglo-American imperialists", "Titoist agents", "traitors to the country", etc.

Our statement to the congress shattered the façade of unanimity by suggesting that the one-sided political activities of the IUS were not liked by British students, and that there might be faults on both sides in the cold war. For this we were accused of "splitting student unity" and misrepresenting British students. For pointing to the fact that Russia,

Poland and other Communist countries were spending money on armaments, just as Britain and America were, we were accused of "slandering the Soviet Union" and putting forward the arguments of the "former Hitlerite youngsters".

From time to time the proceedings were stopped for "spontaneous" demonstrations against our delegation. Chanting such slogans as "Hands off Korea", "Hands off Malaya", "Long live peace", "Stalin, STALIN, S-T-A-L-I-N", etc, hundreds of highly emotional delegates would press round our table for anything up to half an hour. At times they verged on the hysterical, but no attempt was made by the chairman to stop them. Describing our reactions, Lidove Noviny, an objective champion of the Czech press, wrote: "The English and Scottish students were the only ones who remained seated and pretended that they were interested only in newspapers a week old or in stuffing their pipes. A mass of progressive students gathered round the two tables of the British delegation and an African student, waving his hands for silence, said to them: 'You ought to be ashamed of yourselves, you students and young people, who are sitting in your places like paralysed dodderers. Shame on you.' And then all the students sang, in many languages the Anthem of Democratic Youth to the British Delegates."

Thus the British and western heretics became scapegoats who provided a useful target for pent-up emotions. But there was also need for some more positive manifestation and so a spot of solidarity was arranged. Everybody, from the prime minister of Czechoslovakia downwards, came to give greetings from the rostrum. At frequent intervals, professors and peasants, shock-workers and athletes, tram-drivers and bishops, young pioneers and old women, all paid their tribute.

"Long live the fighters for peace, at the head of whom stands our great leader Stalin," said a Catholic bishop. "We know the Defenders of Peace. We shall help them," screamed a ten-year-old pioneer. "We refused to unload American munitions," boasted a French docker.

Then came the gifts for the delegates: an ambulance, driven up the aisle, for the Koreans; a motorcycle for the Chinese; a bust of Stalin for the Albanians; for the British a clock, a cut-glass dish and some gramophone records.

The president of the congress was Alexander Shelepin, at the time he was head of Komsomol, the main Communist youth organisation in the Soviet Union. He was a vice-president of the IUS and later became the head of the KGB, the Stalinist secret police.

Shelepin made a vicious attack on Stanley Jenkins, the NUS president, after he had addressed the congress. He said "Yes Mr Jenkins and Mr Rust, you are traitors to your own people. You help to get Britain transformed into the 49th State of America. When you attack the Soviet Union you act as the enemy not only of the Soviet people but of the British people as well." The speech was followed by 30 minutes of applause.

I had a minor clash with Shelepin at a meeting of the steering committee of the congress. Our delegation had become seriously concerned at the demonstrations that were staged against them following the "spontaneous" appearance at the rostrum by various workers and other groups, so I was asked to raise this issue at the steering committee, which Shelepin chaired. I said that in view of the demonstrations which were being made against our delegation we would appreciate it if we could be told when the "spontaneous" presentations were likely to take place. Shelepin said I could move a motion calling for such a timetable, which I proposed immediately. He then asked if I had a seconder and looked cynically around the room knowing full well that there would be no such seconder. Nor was there one.

There were 20 of us in the NUS delegation to the Prague congress and when we made our report to the NUS conference we recommended that the NUS should disaffiliate from the IUS. We felt confident that when they learned what we had gone through in Prague, and in view of the earlier protests against actions of the IUS leadership, the conference would strongly support disaffiliation. To our utter astonishment, the recommendation was defeated. We could not believe that the majority of NUS members would want in any way to condone the treatment we had received, though we knew that the Communists and their fellow travellers would have no qualms about approving of what happened to us. After all, two of them from the fellow-travelling Student Labour Federation had rushed to the podium to criticise Stanley Jenkins, the NUS president, and both were carried triumphantly round and round our delegation's table.

It was, of course, suggested that some of those who had voted against our recommendation to disaffiliate did not approve of the way we had been treated but felt after their experience of the war that nothing was more important than trying to prevent another war by building links and friendship with the students of other countries, and especially with those living under Communist regimes. One might feel that that showed a naivety that did them credit, but naivety it certainly was. For it showed a failure to recognise that whatever its origins might have been, the IUS had become what I described as "the student branch of the Cominform". It was not a genuine student organisation; it was totally under the control of the Cominform and the Stalinists. And some of its principal leaders were far from being typical students, though they were able, I had no doubt. Alexander Shelepin, the head of the Komsomol, went on to become head of the KGB (though he eventually ended up in Siberia, as some Stalinists were apt to do). Joseph Grohman, the IUS president, was a leading Czech figure, who was later imprisoned following the Slansky trials. Bernard Berenou, a leading member of the IUS executive, later represented Romania at the UN, while Jiri Pelikan, who later became IUS president, eventually fled to the west and became a European MP. One of his fellows on the IUS executive, Jacques Vergès, became a leading advocate in France and defended, among others, the notorious Nazi, Klaus Barbie.

Given the slavish adherence to the Cominform line of the leaders of the IUS and its sister organisation the WFDY (World Federation of Democratic Youth), and the substantial resources which must have been devoted to their congresses and festivals, propaganda, and other activities, I was surprised that when Jeremy Isaacs did his excellent TV series on the Cold War he gave virtually no attention to the efforts of the two organisations to mobilise support for the Communist cause on a worldwide basis.

Whether or not Isaacs and other sections of the media subsequently recognised the significance of what was being done by the IUS, at the time my supporters and I in the NUS certainly did, yet even when we had pointed out such aspects of the IUS and other features of its subservience to the Communist cause, the would-be "bridge builders" could not be convinced of the need to leave the IUS and the vote against that was carried by 757 votes to 622. Following the vote, Stanley Jenkins and all but three of the executive resigned (myself included).

In the run up to the congress I had been one of the principal critics of the IUS at NUS conferences, and in that I had a valuable ally, Andy Sharf who was the finest orator I ever heard in NUS debates. A one-time Trotskyist, he had urged Indians to strive for independence while he was in the British army, so he didn't lack guts! We would have tried to redouble our efforts to show why the NUS should disaffiliate from the IUS, but fortunately the conference went on to decide that there should be a referendum on the issue, and in light of that decision Jenkins and the rest of us returned to the executive.

When the referendum was held in the individual student unions the members voted for disaffiliation from the IUS. Had that not happened I feel sure that the whole future of the NUS would have been threatened.

While the union did not give up entirely its efforts to keep some links with the IUS, its main effort was then directed to creating new ways of spreading international links between students on a basis completely different from that represented by the IUS. The NUS worked with the Swedish NUS to create a new framework and I worked with Olof Palme, their president (who later became prime minister of Sweden) to draw up proposals which we later submitted to a conference of national unions, but not attended by the IUS. That resulted in the establishment of what became known as the International Student Conference to which was attached a co-ordinating secretariat (COSEC) with the purpose of promoting co-operation and joint activities and discussion of issues of national concern but divested of the Communist influence which had permeated the IUS. My predecessor as president of the NUS, John Thompson, became head of the secretariat and subsequently, after working for a time with me on the NUT's national education and careers exhibition, went to work for the World Confederation of Organisations of the Teaching Profession (WCOTP) which he served as secretary-general until his untimely death in a car accident in 1981.

These developments meant that when I became president of the NUS in 1952 a major divisive issue had been brought to an end and, although I led a final NUS delegation to an IUS congress in Warsaw in 1954, the main energies of the union could be concentrated on the domestic issues which were the principal concern of the bulk of the membership.

Of those concerns, the foremost related to grants and welfare. Although many students in the early post-war years were in receipt of grants under the government's FETS scheme and were relatively well catered for, the provision for younger students entering higher or further education straight from school was often very unsatisfactory or sometimes non-existent. Dealing with that problem therefore became a major priority for my executive, and in that connection we were very fortunate in having the services of Stella Greenall, an outstanding official who established a national reputation for the union and herself on all matters relating to grants and welfare. She worked closely with my first deputy president, George Semmens, a tough negotiator who later became a very successful comprehensive school head. The quality of the union's work, research and campaigning in this field led to an important success when the new education minister, David Eccles, recognised the NUS for consultation purposes. Our work in this field also required a great deal of investigation of the provisions made by the local education authorities and national and local campaigning highlighting the injustices that existed in various parts of the country.

One injustice of a different kind arose from the treatment of an individual student in a teacher training college which we succeeded in making something of a *cause célèbre,* and led to a marked improvement in life in those colleges. It arose in 1952 from the expulsion of Sheila Davies, the president of the student union in Bangor Normal training college in North Wales, after she had written to the NUS making known her criticism of the college's disciplinary code, and for leading a demonstration of her members over it. On learning of the way she and her students had been treated we organised a letter-writing campaign to MPs and managed to secure an adjournment debate in the House of Commons. That led to a statement from the minister of education saying that the college was wrong to do what it did. Sheila Davies was reinstated at another college and went on to achieve a master's degree and a successful teaching career. It also enabled us to open up the whole issue of the attitude of training colleges to their students, an attitude that would not be tolerated if adopted in the universities. From that point on, the situation in the colleges improved.

When carrying out the campaign I was approached by the National Union of Teachers which was, understandably, very interested in the case, and offered to take the matter over. I thanked the union for its offer but said I thought we could handle it ourselves, though we would let it know if we needed any assistance. That was my first direct contact with the union, and I have an idea that it had a bearing on my future appointment as an NUT official.

In what was to be an exhilarating two years as president there were a number of experiences which I shared with others and greatly valued. One of those was the organisation of the National Student Debating Tournament. I had been struck when attending debates at the Oxford Union that while the general level of debating there was good and sometimes excellent (though hardly impromptu) it was no better and often not as good as much of the debating I heard at NUS conferences and in individual student unions. I felt that students generally could benefit from the cultivation of the art of debating which could come from the opportunity to debate with speakers from other universities and colleges. I therefore approached David Astor, the editor of the *Observer,* to ask if his paper would be willing to sponsor a National Student Debating Tournament. Encouraged by his colleague Kenneth Harris, one of the wittiest debaters I ever heard at Oxford, Astor agreed to the sponsorship. The paper paid for a handsome silver mace to be awarded to the winning team, and Kenneth and I were charged with devising the rules for the tournament and selecting the venues and judges.

The first final was televised by the BBC and, thanks to a technical hitch somewhere, we had an extra ten minutes on air when I was able to ad lib on the merits of the NUS. The first winner of the mace was Ruskin College, one of whose team was Bill McCarthy who later became a fellow of Nuffield College, a leading expert on industrial relations and trades unions and a Labour peer, who sadly died recently after a long illness. The tournament ran for several years under the auspices of the NUS and the *Observer,* and later was taken over by the English Speaking Union.

Apart from the drama and oppressive nature of the participation in the IUS congress in Prague, I was able to benefit from enjoyable trips to Stockholm, Istanbul, Copenhagen, Belgium, France, Warsaw and Madrid. The most fascinating, and in some respects frightening, experience came when I led an NUS delegation to the Soviet Union in 1954.

The trip lasted three weeks and took us to Leningrad, Kharkov, Yerevan and to Moscow where we attended the May Day parade in Red Square and a banquet in the Kremlin. We had discussions with many students and activists, a group of writers and artists who included a celebrated satirist, Mikhail Zoshchenko, who had been attacked by the Communist Party leadership. We also had a three hour meeting with the Soviet minister for higher education, Mr V.P. Elyutin. The meeting was gruelling and at times had an Orwellian flavour which is shown by the extract from an article

I wrote for the *Observer* on my return from Moscow. In it I said:

> Somebody put another question to the Minister. "Our students always like to have the facts," replied Mr Elyutin, sharply. "They are against somebody imposing false, second-hand opinions upon them."
>
> "Then shall we be able to read and see pictures of Trotsky's part in the Revolution?" I asked.
>
> "For that it is necessary to reveal the facts which show the role and quality of Trotsky in the Revolution," the minister replied.
>
> One of his subordinates joined in. "Trotsky had always been a traitor. History has already proved that," he said, as though he were reciting a mathematical formula. "Our students know that Trotsky was a traitor and an enemy of the people and none of them will wish to read of him," added the deputy minister for higher education, who was also present.

A discussion I had subsequently with a postgraduate was even more Orwellian in flavour. I wrote:

> One night in our hotel at Kharkov I asked Jiri, a 30-year-old history postgraduate who was attached to the delegation as a guide, if he had believed the accusations made against Beria.
>
> "Of course," he replied, "I am convinced he was a spy."

"But do you think he was a spy for 30 years? How could he possibly escape detection for so long and reach such a powerful position?" I asked.

"Because he was a very clever spy."

"If it is possible for a spy to become a member of the Soviet war cabinet and be appointed deputy prime minister by Mr Malenkov, do you think any of the present government might be spies?"

"No," he replied. "They are all known and trusted by the people."

"But wasn't Beria known and trusted too? Wasn't he a 'great leader' according to *Pravda*?"

"No. Beria was never a great leader. Only Stalin was a great leader. Beria only took office in 1938."

"Aren't you at least a little disturbed that such a thing happened?"

"No. I am glad because it shows the strength of the Party."

In light of those encounters and what we saw in the course of our trip, and my own battles within the NUS itself, it was not altogether surprising that one of my contemporaries, Chris Price, who became a Labour MP and, later, director of Leeds Polytechnic, should tell the *Times Educational Supplement* that I was "a remarkably tough and scathing critic of the pro-Moscow British Communists who were threatening to take over the NUS". Mark you, I could be equally scathing about Tories too (see Student days) but there were not many of them about in the NUS in my time.

I might add that I found it very disquieting when visiting Yalta in 1989, as a guest of the Russian teachers' union, that the young Russians I talked to were anything but enthusiastic about Gorbachev's introduction of *glasnost* and *perestroika*. The roots of Stalinism had clearly sunk deep.

I have referred to some of the leading figures in the IUS, their attitudes and their service to a cause I abhorred, and actions I condemned. But one of the most gratifying aspects of my involvement in the NUS was the opportunity it also gave me to meet and work with student leaders from other countries I respected and admired and with whom I had, or continue to have, a warm friendship. Of those friends there was one who became an outstanding figure, not only in his own country but on the world stage.

Olof Palme became prime minister of Sweden and held that position when he was murdered by a still unknown assassin in 1986, an enormous loss not only to his own country but to world affairs as well.

Some months before he was killed he wrote this letter, which I treasure as a reminder of his optimism and dedication and humour.

Dear Fred,

Usually I have received a card from you at Christmas time then I have spent the time to Easter to decipher – without quite succeeding.

This time I had decided to be a better letter writer, but as usual I didn't get around to it.

But now the first free weekend of the year, three days after the presentation of the budget, I feel free to expose you to my hand-writing.

Politically, times have been tough in so far that we are trailing in the opinion polls and have an election coming within eight months. But this is the after-effect of a lot of unpopular economic measures. In fact we have succeeded much better than we ever hoped for to bring order to the economy. Unemployment is down to 3.8%, inflation is coming down, production is increasing, foreign trade is in balance, and the budget deficit is diminished without any cuts in the fundamental measures of the welfare state. So we may very well succeed in winning.

I am dismayed at everything I read about the miners' strike. It is terrifying because it is so clearly a part of a pattern to undermine the trade union movement.

Personally, we are quite well. Lisbet and I have moved into the Old Town, five minutes away from my office and three minutes from Parliament. Our oldest, Joakim, who works at the Institute for Fiscal Studies (comparing British and Swedish welfare systems), has taken over the house in Vällingby. Our youngest, Mattias, still lives with us.

Hope all is well with you and your family and the teachers' union.

Olof.

After his death I wrote this obituary for *Education.*

Only a madman, or a zealot for the most vile of causes, could have assassinated Olof Palme. For throughout his career, from his student days when he and I worked together on the international plane, to his premiership, he was, above all else, a passionate believer in the power of reason and the need to persuade by argument. He abhorred violence in any form and dedicated much of his life to promoting international understanding and peace among nations.

While he was a controversial politician within Sweden itself, arousing both fervent support and determined opposition, his contribution to Swedish political life was profound and I cannot believe any Swede fired the assassin's bullet.

The wish to identify with, and walk freely amongst, his fellow citizens which was to cost him his life was indicative of another of his great qualities – he was the truest of democrats. Particularly gifted in so many ways, he was at ease in any company and there surely cannot have been a more relaxed or approachable prime minister anywhere in the world.

He was witty and could show great charm, but when one saw the glint in those piercing eyes one could tell also that there were issues on which he would brook no compromise.

Although he held ministerial office for nearly 20 years he never lost the radicalism which I encountered when, after he had served as president of the Swedish National Union of Students, he insisted that improvement in university student grants had to take second place to providing financial support to school pupils in order that working class children should have a better chance of higher education.

He had his disputes with the Swedish teachers, both during his period as minister of education and when prime minister, as he did with other sections of Swedish society from time to time – but I know my teaching colleagues in Sweden are as shattered by his death as all his many friends in this country and throughout the world. Mankind has lost a unique statesman and the Swedes have lost a controversial, charismatic, but greatly respected prime minister.

Sadly, another good friend of mine was also murdered, not by an unknown assassin but by someone who had worked with him in the civil rights movement in the USA. Al Lowenstein had been president of the National Student Association of the USA before he became involved in politics, when he was elected to the House of Representatives and, later, led the "Dump Johnson" campaign. Another charismatic and dynamic and immensely likeable figure, and again one whose early death was a great loss to political life.

I think all of us who have been or continue to be involved in the student movement should be proud of its ability to produce men and women of such quality, who enrich their society and the world at large.

Clearly, leading the NUS isn't all a bed of roses and there are times when you can get an unpleasant shock. Mine came in connection with NUS travel. For years the union had been winning plaudits for its highly successful travel ventures, having already been successful in that field in the pre-war years. Thanks to a young and dynamic manager, Harry Baum, it took the lead in organising charter flights from which thousands of students benefited, and promoting popular student tours and exchanges. However, Harry moved on to promote his own travel business and some time later his successor greeted me with the news that the union had lost £20,000 on the year's operations. It wasn't the happiest day of my life and we were soon looking for a new manager. Not long after that a young man called to see me to ask whether the union would be willing to back him in a new student magazine he was launching. He was bright and charming but I had to tell him that I had recently launched a news-sheet for union members so the answer had to be "no". The young man's name was Richard Branson – just think what might have happened if he had become our new travel manager!

While the decision to disaffiliate from the IUS and the attempt to build a new framework for international student co-operation brought an end to the bitter divisions of the late '40s and early '50s, there was another issue that caused division in NUS conferences. That arose from the provision in the NUS constitution that the organisation should confine its discussions and actions to those matters which concerned "students as such". There were those on the left who sought to remove that limitation on the grounds that virtually everything affects "students as such" and it was therefore unrealistic to try to prevent discussion of all manner of things beyond grants and welfare, university and college policies, international student co-operation, travel and exchanges, and matters of that kind.

Before and during my presidency we succeeded in maintaining that limitation for a variety of reasons, but primarily because to open up discussion in the NUS to a whole range of political and social issues which concerned all citizens and not only students and education would probably lead to dissent in the organisation and a dissipation of its resources into areas that were less directly related to the welfare and concerns of students in those straitened times. The "as such" clause was wrongly described as a "no politics" clause. It was not, for it did not preclude the discussion and taking of political action on those matters which were of direct concern to or stemmed from the experience of students, and which the public and policy-makers would therefore be prepared to take seriously. Some years later the "as such" clause was deleted. I have my doubts whether it has benefited the union.

Following my presidency and after I had become an officer of the NUT I was responsible for maintaining relations between the two organisations and continued to attend NUS conferences. Much later I became a trustee of the NUS and in that capacity for 20 years or so I was kept in touch with the life and work of the union and from time to time attended NUS conferences and other events, and through all of that time and still today I have a great affection and regard for the union, its membership, its leadership and its staff.

On a number of occasions over the years at NUS conferences, I have heard some critics alluding to the union's leaders as "political careerists". I suppose that leaders in all sorts of organisations get labelled by some critics in such terms – it goes with the territory. But such labelling is both stupid and derogatory to the NUS itself. For it fails to recognise both how important the NUS is and how rich is the experience and level of responsibility that it gives to those who direct and organise its affairs, and which can enable those who have benefited from them to give service and expertise to a wide variety of organisations, businesses and causes. And while some former leaders have gone on to prominent political careers like Jack Straw, Charles Clarke, and Jim Murphy, many have gone in other directions.

Those who served with me in the executive of 1952-54 have included a head of a TV company, a chief executive of a major city, a successful barrister, a key scientific adviser to governments, a world authority in the petroleum industry, a publisher and advertising executive, and a success-ful head teacher. Over the succeeding years I am sure the same story applied and members of the NUS over the generations should take pride in what they have created and sustained over more than 90 years.

It is, moreover, an organisation which has been built up and led not by a bunch of toffs from elitist public schools, blessed with rich parents and bathed in privilege, but by the products of the nation's schools and colleges, from all sorts of backgrounds, working together both in the individual student unions throughout the country and in a national body which learns from its experiences and successfully responds to change.

I believe the role of their organisation could become even more important in the years ahead: if I see one serious danger, it is a clash of the generations, with some politicians trying to set the young against the old, pointing to the debts, the hardships, the unemployment and other problems which students and non-students alike may face, while the older members of an ageing population allegedly benefit from pensions and benefits that are falsely described as better than those of their counterparts in other countries. The future of this country will depend on the old and the young joining together to tackle the problems and build a just society, and a strong and wisely-led NUS should play a vital part in that enterprise.

Change at the NUT

As the end of my two-year term as president of NUS approached, I had to consider what kind of job I might seek. There were few openings for "special advisers" in politics in those days, and my other main interest was journalism. I had hopes of that following my Forces Diary column in the *Wallasey News,* the reports I'd done for the local paper, my articles in *Isis* and, most importantly, my article on Russia in the *Observer.* Those hopes were dashed, however, after a discussion I had with Sidney Elliot, the then editor of the *Daily Herald.* In those days of very thin papers, as he put it, "if you haven't got a union card you won't get a job and if you haven't got a job you won't get a union card"!

So I tried the BBC – I had done quite a few broadcasts when at the NUS – and had an application in to be an Outside Broadcast Producer. I actually got as far as an interview for that and appeared before the snooty and pompous Peter Dimmock. When he asked me if I had any ideas for future outside broadcasts I said I thought snooker and darts had good possibilities. By the look on his face when he heard that you'd have thought he had trodden in something – so that was a non-runner.

I had applications in for two other BBC jobs and was enduring the usual long delay before there was any reply, when I had a call from the NUT. Would I be able to see the general secretary, Ronald Gould? Intrigued, I said yes and saw him the next day. Ronnie said that the union was a creating a new assistant secretary post to deal with publicity and press relations, and asked if I would be interested in it. He said he could not offer me the post because it was being advertised and there was likely to be strong competition. I said I greatly admired the union's campaigning for greater educational opportunities for all, and that I would be pleased to apply – and that I felt I could do the job.

Since I had no previous involvement with the union other than my discussions with its representatives when the NUS was running the campaign for Sheila Davies at Bangor Normal College, I assumed the job would go to a union executive member, or a local association officer or a journalist. On the other hand, perhaps the success of our campaign for Sheila may have been the reason for Ronnie's call. So I was astonished when, following my appearance before the whole executive, I was offered the job.

A few days later I got letters from the BBC inviting me to interviews for the two jobs for which I had applied. It was great replying telling them just what I thought of the BBC's arrogance as an employer (those were the days before the arrival of ITV) acting, after great delay, as if it was doing me a favour even acknowledging receipt of applications.

And so it came to pass, as they say, that I became the youngest official at the headquarters of Britain's biggest and best teachers' union. Unlike all the other officials, except the solicitors, I was the only official who had not been a teacher or an NUT member and in my job I could have a wide remit not limited by the need to work for the implementation of particular conference or executive decisions, though of course having a responsibility, when necessary, to explain those policies and decisions to the public. My work involved co-operating with all departments and the regional offices and working particularly closely with the general secretary.

In the first few years I did not have a department but, following the success of the National Education and Careers Exhibition and a number of other early projects, the executive decided that a publicity and PR department should be created (the first of any union in the country) and appointed me head of it, as a senior official.

What was especially pleasing and encouraging on taking up my post was the extent to which my colleagues, and specially the general secretary, were prepared to trust my judgment, back my ideas and, with the executive's support, provide considerable resources for projects I proposed. I was, after all, a complete newcomer; I was not professionally experienced or trained in journalism or public relations. I had not been a teacher – my limited experience of tutoring at Oxford did not remotely compare with the daily tasks of any school teacher – but I did feel strongly about the value of education to every child and young person, to each community, to our society, and to our country. And apart from my war service all my working life and time had been involved in education, and within the NUS exercising considerable responsibilities on behalf of many recipients of education. I imagine it would also have helped that in effect I had been what is today called "head-hunted" for the job, after Ronnie Gould asked me to see him. I guess he must have thought I had done some useful things at the NUS.

My first NUT conference was at Scarborough in 1955 (I've attended another 60 since then!) and after it Ronnie Gould asked me if I had any suggestions to offer. Apart from commenting on what I sensed was the growing anger and frustration teachers were feeling about their pay and conditions, I thought there were two things the union ought to do. The first was that all conference sessions (except the finance session) ought to be open to the press. Until then, journalists were only allowed to see a few sessions and naturally most of them sought to find out what happened in the closed sessions. That suggestion was quickly accepted.

The other was rather more tricky. I suggested that the conference would seem more workmanlike if the platform was occupied only by the officers, executive members, and officials when necessary, and that apart from the opening session and the presidential address, the wives of the officers and executive members should be seated somewhere else. I was treading on a few toes in suggesting that, but it was agreed to.

There were a number of other ways in which I made suggestions for change as I got into the job. Probably the most significant, outwardly at least, was to improve the union's image by changing the logo and the design of all its publications and notepaper. I did not consult any committee, though I did tell the general secretary, and secured the services of Harold Bartram, a lecturer in design at the London School of Printing. So out went the respected but ancient figures that were on what constituted the logo and in came the flaming torch. The fee we paid Harold for the logo was vastly smaller than that paid to the designer of what was, in my view, the inferior logo which was introduced upon my retirement, but much of his restyling of the union's publications lasted for many years. Moreover, the changes he made were welcomed without any complaints by executive members and colleagues alike.

Another change which I considered necessary, and which was agreed to, was to introduce graduates and specialists into the union's staff. Until then, most recruits came to the union straight from school and began work in the dispatch department before moving elsewhere. Although I was allocated an excellent chief clerk in Bob Shepherd, I proposed that for our press and PR work it was essential to have recruits who had experience in journalism, public relations, publicity, or exhibition organisation. This was accepted, and as our needs expanded so a team of such recruits was employed. During my 15 years in charge of the union's publicity and PR I had the help of some quite outstanding colleagues, among them Toni Griffiths, Stuart Skyte, John Hall, and Janet Davidson. And it has been especially pleasing that one of my team, Rita Donaghy, went on from the union and eventually became a president of the TUC, chair of ACAS, and is now a member of the House of Lords.

In the years that followed, other departments in the union's headquarters and regional offices also brought in specialists in various fields, many of them graduates. Their predecessors in earlier times, judging by those I worked with in my early years at Hamilton House, would surely have gone to university or college in their youth had they enjoyed the same opportunity for higher or further education as subsequent generations.

Aiming high and seeking quality

Years later, commentators were kind about some of the things I did in the course of my work at Hamilton House. One said: "The NUT's sleek publicity operation is regarded as a model in the trade union world." Another said: "Jarvis's managerial role at the NUT is unchallenged. The NUT became smoothly identified with the 1960s expansion and modernisation of schooling."

It is for others to judge whether such comments are justified, but what I do know is that in approaching my work at the union and throughout my 35 year career with it I took the view that nothing was too good for children and teachers and education; that in whatever we attempted to do on their behalf we should always aim high, and seek to secure and use the best quality talent and expertise. So, for example, when we organised the first National Education and Careers Exhibition we engaged a top architect and a leading industrial designer to create it and invited the Queen to be its patron and open it; to make the case for greater investment in education we enlisted the help of leading businessmen and public figures; when we launched the biggest campaign for education the country has ever seen we invited the prime minister and the leader of the Opposition to address it and some 170 distinguished public figures to become patrons of it; in carrying out a survey of the condition of the nation's schools we employed the services of one of the country's top opinion and market research agencies; when we organised a major national conference on the media and popular culture the speakers included the home secretary and outstanding authorities in those fields; and when we established an education and training centre we acquired a magnificent stately home, truly worthy of a great profession.

In short, at all times and in whatever we endeavoured, we should go for top quality, never for the second-rate. Fortunately, in striving to do that we invariably had the backing of a forward-looking executive and a willing membership. In the pages that follow I hope it will be seen that, while there was always more we might have done, we were successful in a variety of directions.

Relating to the media

While, for the most part, I saw my task in the newly created post as developing the union's public relations as well as its press relations, and I was given every support in that approach, I always saw my first priority as communicating the union's policies, views and activities to the public through the press, radio and TV and via our own publications. Before I started at Hamilton House the union's press releases were issued through the union's library and any queries were dealt with by the librarian, Wyn Shelley, and her colleague Bob Shepherd, both excellent, experienced members of staff. Bob was transferred to my office and gave me tremendous support until his retirement.

In those early days there were few specialist education correspondents. The pioneers were Dinah Brooke *(Observer)*, Kay Gibberd *(Sunday Times)* and Paul Cave *(Daily Mirror)*. I had known Dinah and Kay during my time at the NUS and developed a very good working relationship with them to the point when on one occasion, the union was holding a special conference at Margate which neither could attend, so I arranged to write reports for both their papers, taking care to write them in such a way as to suggest they were not written by the same person but still conveying the essence of what had happened at the conference. With Paul Cave my collaboration was of a different kind: it was to help in the production of an eight-page special feature on education for the *Mirror,* a terrific venture on his part. My friendship with Paul lasted well into his retirement, when I did several photo shoots for his *Hampshire County Magazine.*

Gradually the number of education correspondents increased and in time they formed their own group with which we developed very good relations, though from time to time some of its members could be a thorn in the side of executive members. One of those was Roy Nash *(News Chronicle/Daily Mail)* who seemed to have a knack of getting to know about confidential proceedings. He also visited Hamilton House to go through our press cuttings looking for local education stories that he might pursue.

There was one occasion when, indirectly, Roy did me a good turn. It occurred when the union conference was meeting at Blackpool. One day Roy had to go elsewhere so he arranged for a colleague from the *Mail's* Manchester office to cover for him. When his colleague arrived I briefed him over lunch and then turned to look at the *Sporting Life* to see what horses I might back that day. Seeing this, the journalist asked me if I was interested in horses. I said I was "after a fashion", at which he said he would phone his office to see if he could get any information on that day's racing. When he returned, he gave me the names of two horses (which I will never forget – Fusil and Wymwyn). He said they were at long odds (10/1 and 100/8) and the prices might shorten, but they were "trying to win". I did not know my informant but felt I had nothing to lose (I'd already been losing all that week) so I would back the horses. After telling a colleague, who was also interested in horses, I rushed of to the bookie and backed both horses singly and in combination. When the afternoon session ended I went back to the bookie and was staggered to discover that both horses had won at the original price. It was my best win in years – and judging by the way the bookie slammed the shutters down it certainly wasn't his best day. So I've always had a soft spot for that particular man from the *Mail* – and, indirectly, for Roy Nash too.

I didn't get any help of that kind from any member of the education correspondents group but I and my colleagues on the union's publicity and PR committee did have an enjoyable evening with them every year at conference. We held a special dinner for them and they, in turn, decided to present a cabaret which for years became a regular feature of the evening. The star performers in the cabaret were John Izbicki *(Telegraph)* who did superb Marcel Marceau routines, Bruce Kemble *(Express)*, the poor man's Max Miller, and George Low *(Education)* with a delightful portrayal of a teacher on holiday in Provence.

In time the BBC and ITV appointed their own education reporters, outstanding among whom were the indefatigable David Smeeton (BBC), Mark Mardell (LBC) who is now the BBC's North America editor, Mike Green and Isobel Allen (ITN), and much later the very fine Mike Baker. There was also a long spell when I had many early morning sessions with the great Brian Redhead (BBC's *Today* programme). He wasn't an education specialist but the interviews with him were invariably sympathetic and helpful to our cause.

There are many others in the media with whom I formed warm friendships and very productive working relationships and whose professionalism I admired. I cannot name them all but I must mention Brian MacArthur *(The Times)* and Richard Bourne *(Guardian)* who wrote booklets for the union on the working lives of teachers and, later, *The Struggle for Education,* a lavishly illustrated history of public education, commissioned by the union to mark the centenary of the great 1870 Education Act. Peter Preston, John Fairhall, John Carvel, Wendy Berliner (all of them *Guardian*), John Scott (PA), Stephen Jessel (*The Times* and BBC), John Izbicki, Jim Dawson and David Fletcher *(Telegraph)* were all fine journalists who produced fair and accurate reports. I cannot recall any time in the many years I worked with them when I had reason to complain about what they had written, and there were plenty of occasions to be grateful to them.

In those times and up to my retirement most of the education correspondents were able to get space for longer reports and articles than most of them are able to achieve nowadays and we now see very little in-depth, investigative journalism, which is very regrettable given some of the things that are happening in education today. There are also fewer education reporters and editors and the education correspondents group no longer exists. I do not regard websites and blogs as any compensation, but I guess that dates me.

In addition to the relations I and my colleagues had with the national press (and the big provincial papers' representatives – also sadly reduced in numbers) and radio and TV journalists, I had good and close relations with the specialist education press – the *Times Educational Supplement, Education* and the union's own weekly journal, *The Teacher.* They too had some excellent regular and feature writers and editors who shared our passion for education and sought to chronicle the achievements and problems of schools and colleges and at the same time provided many features of considerable help to the profession. My links to the *TES* went back to the war years, when I first received the encouragement of the great editor Harold Dent, with whom I kept in contact until his death. My friend Stuart Maclure was another outstanding editor, first of *Education* and then for 20 years of the *TES.* Other editors whose help and friendship I enjoyed, and for which I was deeply grateful, were Patricia Rowan, Caroline St John-Brooks, Judith Judd, Bob Doe and Gerard Kelly (all of the *TES*), Tudor David (*Education* and *The Teacher*), George Low (*Education Guardian*), and Nick Bagnall and Peter Singer (of *The Teacher*). All those editors benefited from the talents of some very fine journalists and it has been good to see many of them go on to further success in other fields. It has also been very kind of the editors of all three publications to publish articles and photographs from me over many years, and especially during my retirement.

There are also very talented journalists and feature writers who I had the pleasure of working with over the years and there is one, in particular, to whom I have good reason to be very grateful. She is Anne Corbett, who was the education correspondent of *New Society*. Anne did a magnificent job for me when I was secretary of the Council for Educational Advance when she wrote *Much To Do About Education*, the guide to all the major education reports and which proved to be a best-seller. In later years she also did a splendid job writing about developments in education in the European Union.

As someone who began writing for the local press within weeks of leaving school, and who wrote a column for his local paper while serving in the army, I was pleased that the union always recognised the importance of local and provincial newspapers and valued the coverage which so many of them gave to all aspects of education. Our department gave a lot of help and advice to the union's local officers and many of them had extremely good relations with the local press. Again one must express regret that, with the advance of the digital age and the financial problems of the newspaper industry, so many local newspapers have had to close. In many cases it means that education has lost a valuable ally.

In my retirement I've not had the opportunity to know and work with as many journalists, writers and editors as I did during my 35 years at Hamilton

House. I am however pleased to keep in touch with quite a few of today's writers, and particularly admire the work of Melissa Benn, Fiona Millar, Richard Garner, Warwick Mansell and Peter Wilby, who has an impressive record and who I consider is the best journalist writing about education today. I also greatly value the work and help of Will Woodward (*Guardian*) and Ed Dorrell (*TES*).

There are of course, one or two other writers and journalists who I would rate as my *bêtes noires,* but I wouldn't want to name them. They get enough publicity already.

Voices from outside

1: Investment for national survival

I always felt, and still feel, that some of the most influential advocates for education come, or should be sought, from outside education. After all, the public expects that those who provide education will speak up for it, stress its value, proclaim its achievements and emphasise its needs. "They would say that, wouldn't they" is the reaction one can expect to the words of teachers and their union.

So one of the things I recommended to the general secretary and the executive was that we should go outside the union, to enlist the interest and influence of distinguished figures from business and public life, to investigate the need and call for increased investment in education. We had already staged the National Education and Careers Exhibition with the support of major employers' organisations, and with this new project we could send a message about education directly to the government and the public at large. So in 1961 we established an independent committee to investigate and call for increased investment in education, which led to a report entitled "Investment for

National Survival" – a compelling message from an impressive group.

Having secured approval for the venture, I sought the help of Professor John Vaizey, who was emerging as a leading authority on the economics of education. He agreed to produce the necessary papers for the group together with Simon Pratt, and he suggested some possible members of the committee. It was particularly important to enlist a leading figure from the world of industry and he was able to persuade Sir Hugh Beaver, a former president of the Federation of British Industries (now the CBI), to join the committee together with other leading businessmen. Through our contacts, other key public figures agreed to serve and the vice-chancellor of Leeds University, Sir Charles Morris, agreed to take the chair. At the time, the union was not affiliated to the TUC but its distinguished general secretary, George Woodcock, agreed to serve.

It was a measure of the esteem in which the union was held that such an outstanding committee should be willing to undertake such an important task, and it was creditable that the union should agree that the committee should work completely independently. This was the conclusion of its final report:

Footing the Bill

Whatever the means by which the education system is to be financed in the future, it is clear that if we are to have the sort of expansion which is essential much more money has to be found for the service. We believe the programme of educational development outlined in Appendix 1 represents the possibility of a notable move forward to an adequate, modern education system that a country with our resources and conditions must afford as soon as possible. We say this fully recognising that it implies a sustained and massive effort to recruit teachers for 20 years – and not for a series of emergencies, as has too often been the case in the past – and above all, that the proposals will be expensive.

It is true that this expenditure will pay dividends in terms of our ability to compete internationally, and the betterment of our own society. But in the short run it will be very expensive. We shall have to pay more rates and taxes (even if some of the increased expenditure is met by privately paid fees, it will still represent a sacrifice of other goods and services). There are signs already that there is a tendency to find the bill too large. We cannot believe that this short-sighted attitude is permissible. We have to pay more in the next few years.

In the short run – over the next five years especially – we have to make a big effort which will be relatively greater than the rise in the national income. Our plea is, therefore, for a sense of urgency now, to recruit the teachers, and to pay for a more adequate education service now; for it is our view that the nation has to make its effort now even though it means paying far more.

Looking further ahead, however, we do not believe the task is beyond the capacity of this country. It is necessary for economic growth. When that growth takes place, it will be easier for the nation to pay for its education service. In recent years the proportion of the Gross National Product devoted to education has risen appreciably – last year it was 4.5 per cent, compared with 1.5 per cent in 1921, 2.25 per cent in 1938, and 3.5 per cent in 1955. In our view the rise should continue, but in the long run a wealthy nation can spend its income on a wide range of goods and services without imposing harsh choices on itself.

It is true to say, too, that it is extremely likely that a higher rate of education expenditure now will help the national income to grow faster in the future. So that the faster we spend in the next decade the easier it will ultimately be to provide a really adequate education system. We believe that the discussion is not about the feasibility of each individual reform in the long run but rather about its timing.

To conclude, then, broadly, the choice before us is this: if we expand higher education to yield a gross output of teachers of 30,000-35,000 a year, we can achieve by 1970 all the reforms now proposed, and go on by 1980 to what looks like a luxury, but is, of course, common already to the higher socio-economic groups. To sustain this rate of expansion, however, we have to be prepared not only to expand higher education rapidly (as we will be forced to do anyway because of the pressure for admission) but also to find the finance for an adequate education system. We cannot have it on the cheap. An expansion of at least £50m a year for at least 20 years seems to be a reasonable target from the point of view of society's needs; but it is a heavy burden for public expenditure to bear. We believe this investment must be made.

Signed: Charles Morris (Chairman)
          Richard Bailey
          B.V. Bowden
          Lionel Elvin
          Norman Fisher
          J.A. Hunt
          F.W. Oakley
          C.T. Saunders
          Richard Titmuss
          Michael Young.

Sir Hugh Beaver, who was a member of the Committee, has made the following observations:

I have taken part in the discussions that have led up to this report, and I am most grateful to the NUT for inviting me to do so. I am however not signing the report – not because I find myself in any way opposed to the broad conclusions and recommendations, but because I have not the specialised knowledge and experience that would justify my expressing detailed views on the question of the future national policy of education and its financing.

As it appears to me the broad facts are as follows:

The Government's proposals which are expensive and courageous still will not in any way answer the demands of the future – for two main reasons.

(a) All the indications are that the growth of population and the number of young people requiring education at all stages – primary, secondary, university, technical – will be far greater than anything that has yet been covered (even in plan).

(b) So far as the later stages of secondary education and all university education go there are sources of supply of worth-while material at present largely untapped, e.g. girls and the wage-earning families.

In my opinion the case is undeniable that present plans will be found to be inadequate and that the size of the problem of the provision of teachers has still not been faced.

This is only a minority report in the sense that I have explained above, and I do not think that any of my colleagues on the committee would dissent from my view – although they have of course much more to contribute in regard to the details than I can.

There was a big demand for the report when it was published and it had to be reprinted. It was to provide very useful ammunition for the 1963 campaign which followed.

Voices from outside

2: The Chuter Ede lectures

In keeping with the purpose I had in mind when suggesting that the union should invite a distinguished group of public figures not directly involved in education to examine the need for increased investment in education, I next proposed that we should establish an annual public lecture to mark the outstanding service given by James Chuter Ede to education, public life, and the union.

The lecture was to be different from others in the field of education in that it would be given by a person who was not directly involved in education but who was prominent in public, business or cultural life, and who would look at education from the viewpoint of its importance to our survival as a whole and assess its importance to their own particular sphere of activity.

The first lecture was given by R.A. Butler, the home secretary, who had been the joint architect with Chuter Ede of the 1944 Education Act. He was followed, among others, by Yehudi Menuhin and Michael Tippett. In 1964 the prime minister, Harold Wilson, gave the fifth lecture. In that lecture he paid tribute to Chuter's many qualities and great service. He said:

I have referred to Chuter's loyalty to education. Because though he held some of the highest offices in the land, the senior Secretaryship of State, Leadership of the House of Commons, I think he was disappointed after the war when it was to the Home Office and not to the Ministry of Education that he was sent by Clem Attlee. But he would have as like complained about that or allowed criticism about it as he would have expected a Surrey fielder to object to being placed by the captain at deep extra third man when he wanted to be at silly mid-off. He didn't complain – he got on with the job, but he was once reported to have said, "I can think of no higher post in any government than the Ministry of Education. It is the one Ministry that deals in Hope." In his five years at the Ministry he played his part in seeing that it dealt also in achievement. And in the years that followed, his power in the counsels of government and his wise advice and understanding were always available to those who held the post of Minister of Education.

During his time at the Board of Education his non-conformist background – he was a Unitarian – was an asset in dealing with the denominations over the clauses on voluntary schools. He understood and respected the feelings of his fellow Non-conformists about extending state aid for church schools, but he could see the point of view of the leaders of the denominations and he was on cordial terms with some of their principal spokesmen. The only people to whom his sympathy did not extend were an extreme faction of the Church of England who put in proposals to the Board counter to those of their own Archbishops. And his comment on that was "We would not stand for that in a trade union". His trade union, Mr Secretary, was of course the NUT.

Some years later the series of Chuter Ede lectures came to an end. But now that education is so much the centre of public attention, and the staging of annual public lectures in a variety of fields is growing, I would suggest that there should be consideration of a new series focused on education given, as the Chuter Ede lectures were, by national figures not directly involved in education. If we can have Grayson Perry giving the BBC's Reith Lectures (and very entertaining they were too) why not invite somebody like Dame Helen Mirren to launch the series? Her fine speech at the 2014 BAFTA awards ceremony, with its reference to the great debt she owed to her teacher, and the striking response she received from the stars in the audience, as if they felt they were similarly indebted, is a pointer to the message that a lecture by her could send to the public at large, a message that surely needs to be conveyed.

Taking education to
Olympia and beyond

The biggest single task I undertook before I became general secretary of the union was to devise and direct the National Education and Careers Exhibition at Olympia in 1959. It was the first exhibition of its kind to be staged in this country so there was no precedent to follow. I did go to the great Brussels exhibition to see how it had dealt with education, but it had done very little. Moreover, I had never organised any kind of exhibition and, indeed, had visited very few up to that point, not even the Ideal Home! Nevertheless, I was able to persuade the general secretary and the executive that there was much to be gained by putting education on the map at a major exhibition centre, as one way of demonstrating how vital education is to children and young people and their families, and to show how it could link to future careers.

I said we needed to aim high with such a venture and that it would not come cheap, but that if we could bring in employers to present the careers side that would reduce the cost. In fact the cost to the union was £40,000 – quite a sum in those days, and all the more credit to the union that it was prepared to make such an investment and entrust it to a novice.

But I had also made it clear that we should engage a top designer to create the exhibition and that whenever possible we should involve pupils and students in live demonstrations of their educational activities. It was also agreed that in the careers section we should invite employers' federations or comparable bodies to promote the careers and opportunities available in a whole industry, service or profession, rather than individual employers. The employers agreed with that approach and we had an excellent response over a wide field of employment.

With these features determined, I then proposed that we should invite the Queen to become the patron of the exhibition, and to visit it. She accepted both invitations.

We hoped that we could attract school parties from all over the country to come to the exhibition and, again, there was an excellent response. In fact the response was so good that it added considerably to the organiser's problems, for there was little in the way of accommodation or parking facilities at Olympia. Thankfully, I had tremendous help from John Thompson, who had been my predecessor as president of the NUS, and other colleagues. We were equally fortunate in securing the services of one of the country's leading architects, Eric Lyons (he designed Span housing) and one of the country's top industrial designers, Hulme Chadwick, to design the exhibition and organise its construction, and they did a magnificent job.

Thanks to them, we were all set for the opening of the exhibition, and that is when you begin to learn from your inexperience. As I've explained, we wanted whenever possible to have pupils and students doing live demonstrations of their school and college activities, and one of them was to be cooking. Gas ovens were duly ordered and installed, but when we arrived at Olympia on the opening morning all of them had disappeared. It did nothing to ease the shock to be told by regular exhibitors "that always happens at Olympia"! The thieves knew the ins and out of Olympia far better than we did.

Another considerable upset occurred on the day of the Queen's visit. The day before she was due to come I was visited by a detective who needed to check the arrangements for the visit and in particular to study the route Her Majesty would follow as she toured the stands. These were the days long before the ultra security conscious times we now live in, but obviously it was necessary to assure the detective that her tour would be conducted in safety. He was happy with the route planned and I guess it would have been great if we could have followed it. What we had not anticipated was the large crowd of young visitors who would pack all the gangways round the exhibition, and which made it impossible to follow all of the planned route. Thankfully, with the aid of stewards, we did manage to find a path for the Queen and Duke of Edinburgh to follow, cheered on by the youngsters. And we sighed with relief.

Following the success of the national exhibition we then undertook two new ventures. The first, again with the support of leading employers, was to organise an annual convention for teachers doing careers work in schools to be given up-to-date information about employment opportunities and discuss their work with employers' representatives.

The other venture was in the exhibition field. I proposed that we should devise an exhibition on primary education and take it on tour to cities and towns outside London. It was entitled Foundation for the Future and within the framework we created and transported the work of local schools and their pupils was exhibited. We invited Sir Eric James, the head of Manchester Grammar School, to open the exhibition in Norwich, after which it was taken to Northampton, Widnes, Liverpool, Aylesbury, Manchester, Bury, Gateshead, Doncaster, Sheffield, Dagenham, Grimsby and Worthing.

As another part of the union's attempt to show the quality and variety of the work being done by children and teachers, we established an education film library at Hamilton House, with the help of the British Film Institute. The most popular films borrowed from the library by NUT associations and others were the union's three documentaries, *I Want to Go to School, Our School* and *The Happy Adventure.*

In addition to the distribution of films about education, we sought to encourage and promote the making of films by children and young people in their schools and clubs. The union sponsored the Young Film Makers Awards in co-operation with the British Film Institute and the Society for

Education in Film and Television. The winning films and awards were presented at the National Film Theatre. When I told Lord David Puttnam about this venture years later he said, "I am amazed at the ambition you had for young people – a category for film makers under 12! We could certainly do with some of that in the '90s."

Blackboard Jungle tales, and the ration book

Not long after I had started work at Hamilton House the American film *Blackboard Jungle* arrived in this country and was shown in our cinemas. As is their habit, some sections of the media started to run stories to suggest that there was a "blackboard jungle" developing in our own schools. It did not take much of an incident in one or two schools for them to embellish their stories into a cause for public concern.

In order to deal with those stories we carried out a survey by random sample of 10% of all secondary modern schools (this was in the pre-comprehensive era) to which we received an 85% response. In addition, I spent a month visiting schools in a number of big cities. The response of the media to the results of the survey and my visits to the schools was very encouraging, and we succeeded in dispelling the idea that there was any sort of "blackboard jungle" in our schools. We did not, however, seek to conceal the problems that were occurring in a number of schools as a result of the growing shortage of teachers. In one school I visited there had been no less than 30 supply teach-ers employed in a single term, some of them with very limited experience, with, understandably, very unsettling effects on pupil behaviour.

Not long after our survey the ministry of education announced the minister's proposal to deal with the "maldistribution of teachers" which included the imposition of a quota for each local education authority, limiting the number of teachers it could employ. The union had already issued a statement calling on the minister to take urgent steps to increase the supply of teachers, but the imposition of quotas did not deal with that. At best, it was a sticking plaster, but it did give me an idea for bringing home to the public the seriousness of the teacher shortage.

In view of the minister's intention to operate a rationing system for teachers I proposed that we should distribute a ration book to the public. In an exact replica of the all too familiar wartime ration book, we replaced the coupons with facts and figures about the scale of the teacher shortage and the steps needed to overcome it. We distributed more than 100,000 copies of the ration book to our local associations; it went down like hot cakes and we were soon being asked to produce more. We were preparing to meet these demands when the general secretary received a letter from Her Majesty's Stationery Office saying that the union had infringed the government's copyright in producing the ration book and asking that we cease distributing it. The general secretary apologised for our inadvertent infringement of the copyright and said we would not distribute any more ration books. But the rationing of teachers continued.

Popular culture and
personal responsibility

After the Olympia exhibition and before the launch of the 1963 Campaign for Education, the union staged an outstanding national conference to examine the impact of mass communications on present-day moral and cultural standards. The annual conference had passed a resolution expressing concern about the activities and influence of some elements of the mass media and I suggested that since such concern was not confined to educationists it would be appropriate and timely to organise a conference in which the recipients and the providers of the output of the mass media should meet together to discuss the issue. The many expressions of support received from organisations and individuals showed that the union's concern was widely shared, and when the conference was held, at Church House, Westminster, it was attended by large numbers of those engaged in education together with parents, those concerned with the welfare of children and young people, and people involved in the mass media themselves.

On behalf of the union I consulted a number of experts in the mass media and the British Film Institute, and we succeeded in drawing up what was a very impressive array of speakers. With a line-up that included R.A. Butler, Raymond Williams, Huw Weldon, Richard Hoggart, *Daily Mirror* boss Cecil King, Herbert Read and Arnold Wesker, the conference was likely to be seen as significant, and indeed it was.

One direct outcome of what proved to be a very successful conference was that Penguin Books published a Pelican Special edited by Denys Thompson entitled *Discrimination and Popular Culture*. The union itself also devised a number of means of following up the conference.

Into films

I doubt whether any other trade union or professional association has made as many as three
documentary films, and even if they had I would be
surprised if they had managed to get any of the
films shown on TV. But that is something the NUT
achieved 50 years ago. How we did it was unusual,
and worth recounting.

It all began with the struggle the union was
engaged in a few months after I started at
Hamilton House (see Change at the NUT). At a time
when there was growing discontent among teachers over their salaries, the government sought to
impose a 1% increase in their pension contributions. That triggered the first big upsurge of
militancy in the post-war period and to sustain the
union's campaign against the government, and also
against the employers from whom it was seeking
a substantial pay increase, the union's executive
agreed that the president should be allowed to
launch an appeal for a fighting fund to add to the
£100,000 which had already been allocated for
campaigning. One of the activities planned was
a mass lobby of parliament in opposition to the
government's pensions bill. I was responsible for
organising it and there was no doubt that the lobby

was going to be on a massive scale, and the prospect was such that the education minister, David Eccles, and the local education authorities, called on the union to cancel it. They said they were not prepared "to negotiate under duress", as if thousands of teachers were going to storm the Palace of Westminster and tear the place apart. In fact, the only storming that occurred took place at Hamilton House, the union's headquarters.

The call of the government and the employers for the union to call off the lobby faced the union's executive with a very difficult decision, especially as the lobby was just a few days away and many associations around the country had made travel plans to attend. The difficulty facing the executive was increased by the fact that the education minister had said the teachers could get the money to pay the increased pension contribution from the Burnham Committee, the body where the employers and unions negotiated teachers' pay – a statement that infuriated the employers but encouraged the union to increase its pressure.

A special meeting of the executive was called to consider these developments and news of it led to a big crowd of London NUT members arriving at Hamilton House to lobby the executive. They stormed into the building and were likely to invade the executive chamber, but were diverted to the refreshment room where they trampled on the executive's sandwiches and cakes as members sought to voice their demands.

Finally, after a bitter debate and by a narrow majority, the executive decided to call off the lobby.

The following day, the BBC's *Tonight* – the corporation's main current affairs programme – invited the general secretary to take part in a discussion with teachers about the dispute and the cancelled lobby. Ronnie Gould accepted the invitation and asked me to go with him. As soon as we got to the studio I could see the "teachers" were mainly the usual suspects, militants from the London area and not a broad cross-section of NUT members. But even if they had been, I've no doubt the mood among members was such, following the cancellation of the lobby, that we would have had a lively session. It was more than lively, and Ronnie was on the ropes most of the time. The discussion became so animated, and with little attempt by the *Tonight* producer to secure a balanced discussion, that the programme overran its allocated time by ten minutes, with the studio crew delighted to have such a stirring show.

The whole item was so unbalanced and the lack of control so blatant that the union sent an official protest to the BBC and called on it to make amends. The high-ups in the BBC did not attempt to justify what had happened and when we said they should do something to make amends, the question was how?

Because of what had happened over the lobby, members who had sent donations to the president's fighting fund started to demand the return of their donations on the grounds that there was no fighting. I suggested to the general secretary and the executive that instead of returning the money it should be used to launch a special PR effort on behalf of teachers and education, and that we should make some documentary films and ask the BBC to show them.

We were given very helpful advice by Stanley Reed, director of the British Film Institute (and a former NUT member). He put us in touch with Graphic Films, an important documentary film company whose staff included Karel Reisz, a leading British director. The upshot was that they produced three documentary films for us – *I Want to Go to School, Our School* and *Happy Adventure.* The BBC kept to its word and the first two films were shown at peak viewing times, and went on to win awards. The films were also distributed by the Central Office of Information, as well as through the union's own education film library.

Although the involvement in the *Tonight* show had been painful, in due course it led to a very positive outcome and, moreover, before the films had been made, the union succeeded in getting a better pay deal from Burnham than had been seen in previous years. It was also gratifying that very few members asked for their donations to the fighting fund to be returned when they were told of the way we proposed to use the money.

It is a mark of the quality of the films that when the British Film Institute presented a season of documentary films made by John Krish, hailing him as one of the country's leading documentary makers, one of the films shown was *Our School.*

No to participation in 'teacher participation'

When I became deputy general secretary of the union in 1970 I was also made head of the education department. That department has always been one of the most important at Hamilton House and over the years, in the development of education policies, its research and its publications, has won much respect and gained much influence beyond the union, especially in the last decade.

In my time with the department one of the most interesting projects undertaken was a major consultation on teacher participation in decision-making in schools. With an increasing number of large secondary schools there was also a growth in the demand by teachers for involvement in decision making; and some felt that stretched beyond consultation and led to active sharing in decision-making. Interest in the idea was given impetus with the creation of a college where there was to be formal machinery for participation in decision-making: Countesthorpe College in Leicestershire. Its key feature was a "moot" through which the staff were to take decisions that would normally have been taken by the head teacher. This development in a profession which had hitherto accepted, or had to accept, that the head of a school was the "captain of the ship" was bound to arouse interest, and became a factor in the decision by the union to undertake a major consultation exercise among its members on the subject of teacher participation. A national working party was elected and consultation meetings were organised around the country, and meetings and discussions went on for more than a year.

It was, in my view, an impressive and valuable exercise. Opinions were divided, not only on the need for consultation but also on whether that should be taken to the point where decision-making powers should be given to the staff collectively.

At that time (the early 1970s) there were substantially more head teachers on the NUT executive, and in the membership around the country, than there are today, and their influence had a bearing on the final outcome of the project. The final report by the executive, which was adopted by the 1973 annual conference, set out in some detail the legal and other implications affecting school governance, which would make it difficult to give decision-making powers to staff. It also cited such factors as the considerable difference in the size of schools, the high degree of staff turnover in many schools, the different bases for governance of schools, complicated by the "religious settlement" and the responsibilities of governors and managers as further obstacles that would have to be overcome. But at the same time it emphasised the extent to which consultation of members of staff was already becoming well established in many schools and especially in the larger ones, and the extent to which in many schools there was already devolution of decision-making to members of staff – but in keeping with the ultimate responsibility of the head teacher.

The executive report argued strongly that there should be full consultation of staff and that such consultation should be made mandatory. It did not recommend following the Countesthorpe idea of giving powers to "moots" although it did recognise that in technical and training colleges the creation of academic boards, to which members of staff were elected, had given staff some decision-making powers in certain areas.

While Countesthorpe might have been seen as a trail-blazer at that time it no longer operates on its original basis, but it certainly helped to stimulate discussion on a very important issue – what should be the powers and responsibilities of head teachers and teachers? It is an issue which is still a timely one given all the talk there is about the autonomy of schools and the "freedom" that is said to be conferred by the creation of academies and "free schools".

Another very significant feature of the work of the education department during my time with it was the amount of time given to the union's participation in the work of the Schools Council. The establishment of the council was a very important innovation and led, particularly, to greater involvement of the teaching profession and others in curriculum development and new teaching practices and techniques. It was seen as a means of opening up the "secret garden of the curriculum" and to the sharing of ideas and relations between schools, teachers, researchers and others.

It was a very sensible and welcome development and the union took its work very seriously. I guess it was too seriously for some politicians – because they felt we had too much influence in its work and in time it was shut down by Keith Joseph in 1982. The folly of that step has been demonstrated in subsequent years, for increasingly nowadays we hear of the importance and value of schools working together in partnerships, federations, etc. Yet that is precisely the kind of co-operation which the Schools Council helped to promote, together with the teachers' centres that grew up around the country in those more enlightened times. Sadly, most of those have been closed too.

Acquiring a stately home

One of the biggest developments during my time as the general secretary was the decision of the executive to acquire Stoke Rochford Hall. It is the biggest and best education and training centre of any trade union in Britain, and I doubt if there is one that can match it in the whole of Europe. But its acquisition was partly due to chance.

It arose from a visit I had paid to what was then the Kesteven training college in 1977. I had been asked to give the last in a series of memorial lectures to mark the role of W.W. Warmington as the principal of the college. The college itself was one of those that were created in the post-war expansion of teacher training provision to meet the growing need for more teachers. Stoke Rochford Hall is a "stately home" near Grantham in Lincolnshire which had been taken over during the war and used in connection with the planning of D-Day. To meet the need to house a substantial number of students, new accommodation was built in the 28-acre grounds together with a swimming pool, and the premises served the purpose well. However, with the subsequent planned contraction in the provision of training places, the college was due for closure soon after I went up to give the last memorial lecture.

After the lecture we gathered for refreshments and talk got around to speculation about what would now happen to Stoke Rochford Hall and the attached buildings. Local guests expressed concern that with the premises on the market they might fall into the "wrong hands". That gave me an idea. For years I had thought of the value of the union having its own training centre. I had seen such a centre years before when I visited Sweden with the help of Olof Palme. He had taken me to a centre outside Stockholm which was imaginatively designed and, needless to say, beautifully furnished.

Stoke Rochford would be quite different, but potentially just as good as the centre I had seen in Sweden. Fortunately, the then union treasurer, Ben Johnson, lived nearby and knew the college well. So on my return to London I told him it was on the market and that we were not likely to get a better buy than Stoke Rochford at what I learned was likely to be the going price. I said that I would have inquiries made about other possible site to see if there was anything available at a comparable price. There was not, and the treasurer was prepared to back the venture. I made it clear that the size of the hall and student accommodation was such that we would need to cater for use by other unions and bodies in addition to the needs of the union. Since we were already expanding our training activities, using hotels at considerable expense, it would be sensible to base them in Stoke Rochford and invite other unions to do the same. The attractiveness and history of the hall also meant that there was likely to be considerable appeal to local people and organisations for a variety of functions.

With the backing of the treasurer, the proposal to buy Stoke Rochford Hall went to the executive, and although there was some opposition the majority of members supported it.

It is now 30 years since the centre was opened by Len Murray, then general secretary of the TUC, and a host of different activities have been staged and a large number of other bodies have used its facilities, in addition to the union itself.

Sadly, a serious fire in 2005 destroyed very important parts of the building to such an extent that it had to be closed for three years. As a listed building, it had to be restored to its original condition, which required much high quality craftsmanship. The restoration cost £10 million, but equally serious was that the hall lost a great deal of business which it would be difficult to recover as the economic recession was affecting the demand of other organisations for the centre's facilities. However, the increasing attention that is likely to be paid to professional development for teachers, in addition to the new activities and services being developed by the centre, will provide new opportunities to promote the use of Stoke Rochford. I may be a sucker for stately homes but I'm sure that such an attractive and exciting venue is truly worthy of a great profession and a far-sighted union.

And other ventures

In addition to the major undertaking represented by the acquisition of Stoke Rochford Hall, there are other ventures and activities which illustrate the vision and enterprise of the union, and which give the lie to those in the media who seek to portray trade unions as dinosaurs and enemies of progress.

For well over a hundred years the NUT has had close links with Teachers Assurance, one of the strongest of the smaller assurance companies. It reports to the union's annual conference and has NUT representatives on its board, and goes from strength to strength, providing a variety of benefits and services.

Not long before I became general secretary, the union launched another big venture, with the founding of the Teachers Building Society. In my view it required considerable courage to take this step, and there were years when the society faced uncertain times, especially during the period of the credit crunch and the recession – a difficult period for all building societies. But it came through those difficulties, and in its latest report to the union's conference it was recorded that there had been a 27% increase in mortgage lending year on year and a rise of 14% in first time buyers.

Remembering how anxious I was in the earliest days about the prospects for the building society, I was tremendously impressed to learn recently that the Teachers Building Society had received the award for the Best Local Building Society for an unprecedented third year running at the What Mortgage awards.

There are other ventures and services the union undertakes which are never reported in the media, like its long-standing benevolent and advisory services, which are deeply appreciated by thousands of teachers and which ought to be recognised by those commentators who seek only to criticise and misrepresent what a modern union like the NUT has to offer.

Campaigning for education

The NUT had a great deal of experience in campaigning well before I had been appointed and the publicity and public relations department established. It was one of the leaders of the campaign for equal pay for women, had campaigned during the Second World War with the TUC in pressing for a new Education Act, and shortly before I joined its staff had run a highly successful campaign to stop the importation of horror comics. But by the mid-fifties new needs called for new efforts and were to lead to what proved to be the biggest campaign in the union's history, one in which it sought and obtained the co-operation of a host of organisations.

The campaign had its origin in a resolution passed at the union's 1962 conference. When the resolution was considered by the publicity committee I persuaded them that we should seek to bring other organisations into a broad national campaign with a broad set of objectives and with the aim of making education a major issue in the next general election. The executive agreed to the suggestion and to the union providing the secretariat for the campaign if other organisations would join in.

The response to the union's invitation was astonishing. By the time the campaign was launched in January 1963 some 70 organisations had agreed to participate and support the agreed manifesto. They included all the principal bodies involved in education and many others. Some of them no longer exist but most of them do, and in spite of the differences they had on some issues and the fact that some were in competition with others (the teachers' organisations not least among them), they were all willing to join the campaign. Equally astonishing were the number of well known national personalities who were prepared to support the campaign as patrons. They included the Archbishops of Canterbury, York and Liverpool, Lady Albemarle, Dame Peggy Ashcroft, Earl Attlee, Sir John Barbirolli, Lady Violet Bonham-Carter, Lord Boothby, Professor Asa Briggs, Dr Jacob Bronowski, Frank Cousins, Sir Geoffrey Crowther, Lord Denning, the Rt Hon J. Chuter Ede MP, Bryan Forbes, Peter Hall, Barbara Hepworth, Wendy Hiller, Richard Hoggart, Sir Julian Huxley, Yehudi Menuhin, Sir Herbert Read, Ronald Searle, Sir Charles Snow and Felix Topolski.

The campaign was launched on 16th January at a packed meeting in Central Hall, Westminster. The Archbishop of Canterbury, the author of three major education reports, Geoffrey Crowther, Lady Albemarle and Alan Bullock, together with Sir Ronald Gould, were the speakers, and the president of the TUC, William Carron, was in the chair. That meeting was followed by mass meetings in nine regional centres and the year finished with another packed meeting at the Royal Albert Hall which concluded with an excerpt from *Julius Caesar* performed by the newly formed National Youth Theatre.

Given that our aim was to make education a major issue at the next general election, the most significant feature of the campaign was a series of meetings attended by the leaders of the three main political parties, probably the first occasion when a major speech on education had been made by party leaders as opposed to their education ministers or spokespersons.

Over Harold's dead body

The series was not only significant but also brought especially memorable moments. The first was when Harold Wilson, the leader of the opposition, was asked the direct question: "Will the Labour Party abolish all grammar schools?" He replied, "The answer to that, as a former grammar school boy, is over my dead body. There may be some people who think that's worth it, but I don't." It was a reply which Labour's opponents quoted frequently and with relish as the argument over comprehensive education developed.

– and a whisky for Mac

Harold Macmillan's meeting was memorable, at least for me personally, for a very different reason. The day of the meeting was the day when the House of Commons debated the Profumo affair. It was probably the most worrying day for the prime minister in his whole career and I fully expected a call from No 10 saying the PM couldn't come. He was, after all, due to be accompanied by Sir Edward Boyle, his education minister, and he could, quite reasonably in the circumstances, have asked him to deliver the speech. But as the time for the meeting approached and no message came I wondered what I could say to Mr Macmillan when he arrived. "Had a nice day, Prime Minister?" hardly seemed appropriate. What else would be welcoming? I was still uncertain as his car arrived and he stepped into Hamilton House. Before I could say anything, the prime minister said: "Do you think you could get me a scotch?" Panic stations! We were due to take the PM to Ronnie Gould's office, but Ronnie was a Methodist and I knew there would be no whisky there. And there was certainly none in my office, so we had to make small talk with the prime minister while one of my colleagues went in search of scotch. Fortunately he came back quickly with a bottle from Mabel's, the pub across the road.

Mr Macmillan delivered his speech with his usual aplomb, with no hint of the pressure and anxiety he must have undergone earlier in the day. And he could not have been more fulsome in the praise he expressed about the campaign when he said: "I am very glad and grateful to have been given this opportunity to attend this meeting and pay my tribute to this campaign, which is the biggest educational effort, the biggest combined effort, to secure educational advance in this country in all our history."

It is worth recalling what the prime minister had to say in his opening remarks about the role and value of education, with words that some of the politicians who have followed him would have done well to echo, but haven't. He said: "The strength of the nation is based partly at any rate upon education. In Scotland we had learnt that lesson before it was learnt in England. Education to my forebears meant as much as religion, something to be practised, not just something to be endured. And it is in the schools and in the universities that we must find the readiness to question existing practices, to experiment with new methods and both to respect and to challenge tradition. Fortunately this is just about the picture of what is going on; and it is the best hope for the future of our country. Our most valuable national assets are brains, the imagination, the power of creation of our people. And we must not also forget the character of the people. We intend to foster and develop talent, to provide each boy and girl with the best possible opportunity; that is the duty of the government, central or local, to provide. But there is something else if I may be allowed to say so which only the individual teacher can do in the educational field; give each boy or girl at whatever stage a sense that they are not just a cog in a huge machine, but an individual living soul."

And when his education minister, Sir Edward Boyle, spoke he emphasised an important feature of the 1963 campaign – the breadth of its support and, especially, the participation of parents. He said: "I want to begin by mentioning one fact which more almost than any other has impressed me about the 1963 campaign. Most of the people who make their voices heard on education start from a professional standpoint – they are educationalists in one way or another. They are politicians or administrators or teachers; in fact the traditional partnership in the education service. But we are being increasingly reminded in this campaign of a fourth partner who has been roused to new awareness, and that fourth partner is the parents of the seven million children now in schools and of the two million and more who will shortly be arriving there. I think it's this new awareness among parents which has given the 1963 campaign its distinctive force. Admittedly – and I welcome this fact – teachers and other educational organisations have taken a leading part in getting the campaign moving; but surely what makes it quite different from anything that has happened before is that it builds on the educational concern of people in all walks of life for the schooling and training of their own and other people's children. And rightly and properly this campaign seeks to arouse and inform that concern still further."

Sir Edward's recognition of the breadth of support for the campaign was most welcome, and events around the country showed how justified it was. In addition to the packed meeting in Central Hall, the nine regional meetings, the Albert Hall rally and the meetings with the party leaders, there were many local events and a widely supported National Education Week in November. In addition there was widespread use of the NUT's education films.

Although these events were scheduled to finish at the end of 1963, the work of the campaign continued for some years afterwards, being taken up by the Council for Educational Advance, which was supported by a substantial number of the organisations which had come together in 1963 and with the secretariat provided by the union.

It is difficult to assess just how far we succeeded in our aim of making education a major issue in the general election, but it undoubtedly received more attention than in preceding elections and the involvement of the leaders of the three main political parties and the importance they attached to education certainly helped to encourage the campaign's supporters and stimulate the interest of the public.

When the general election took place in 1964 it brought a change of government and the appointment of Anthony Crosland as education secretary. Crosland was probably the best education secretary Labour has produced. His attitude to the grammar schools was markedly different from that of Harold Wilson, and he set out in earnest to promote the development of comprehensive education.

The CEA organised conferences on a number of educational issues and it enjoyed a big success when it published *Much To Do About Education* in 1967. Written by Anne Corbett, the education correspondent of *New Society*, it set out the main findings and recommendations of all the major education reports commissioned by the government since the war – Robins, Crowther, Plowden, Albemarle, and Bullock. This excellent guide was reprinted several times and was especially popular with students training to be teachers. It is a pity that those five education reports were not taken as seriously by the country's politicians. If they had acted on their recommendations and provided the resources to implement them we would have started much earlier to build the world class education system that politicians talk about.

The same applies to the excellent report which was produced some years later by the national commission on education led by Sir Claus Moser. Entitled *Learning to Succeed,* it was another well researched and far-sighted document and was frequently quoted by campaigners as pointing the way to the reforms that should be attempted. More recently there was another very significant report produced by the Cambridge Primary Review, led by Professor Robin Alexander. It was the biggest study of primary education since the Plowden report and was based on a nationwide consultation, and saw extensive follow-up actions.

There was a time when governments would pay serious attention to evidence when they formulated policies and decided which needs should be met, and which innovations would raise educational standards. There was a belief in the value of asking a committee or commission of men and women with experience, achievement, and sound judgment to consult widely and examine in depth an issue requiring action. Unfortunately, those ideas have gone out of fashion. Some politicians occasionally pay lip-service to "evidence based" policy making, but there is little evidence that they are prepared to practise it. More and more, and especially with the coalition government, ministers indulge in headline-seeking, back-of-the-envelope gimmicks and the minimum of consultation with those on whom they are utterly dependent for the achievement of any advance in education.

Of course there are organisations and groups and individuals who continue to campaign on particular education issues and make serious efforts to win public support, often with too little attention from the media, sections of which are too prone to fall for the slick talk and snake oil of the politicians. The efforts of these groups are to be welcomed and need support, and in that I particularly commend the decision of the NUT to set up the Fred and Anne Jarvis Education Award which the union was kind enough to establish following Anne's death. The choice of recipients of the award has been wholly admirable, and each of the campaigners has done outstanding work. To date they have been Margaret Tulloch, Fiona Millar, Michael Rosen, Melissa Benn and Robin Alexander, and I am sure they would agree with me that there has been no greater campaigner for education that the 2013 winner – Malala Yousafzai. There has surely never been a more courageous and inspiring campaigner than Malala and no-one who has had the effect on a world-wide scale that she has had. Think how terrific the impact would be if we had a thousand Malalas speaking out for education around the world, and especially in the countries where education provision is abysmally low, particularly where girls are concerned.

Organisations like CASE, Comprehensive Future, Compass and others have been promoting campaigns for years, and have sought to link with others. The teachers' unions, especially the NUT, have undertaken campaigns on a variety of issues and against education cuts and retrograde policies; and Compass and the NUT are to be congratulated on the commission of inquiry that they set up. But there has been no combined effort on anything like the scale of the campaign we waged in 1963.

In my view, the question to be answered now is: does the situation facing education in this country today warrant a new joint campaign? In 1963 there was a host of organisations and individuals who believed it was necessary to ensure that education became a major issue in the forthcoming general election. Today the need is not to secure attention for education but to prevent the complete fragmentation and possible destruction of our education system and the further widening of the inequalities that exist within it.

As an ageing campaigner it is not for me to answer that question, but I hope that in the light of what I say in the final chapter of this book, those who have the wherewithal to mount a new combined effort will feel the time has come to do just that. I appreciate that some of the organisations which joined together in 1963 no longer exist, and that there are a variety of new campaigning techniques that may warrant different ways of campaigning. I'm sure that I am not alone in thinking that what is at stake for the future of the children, young people and adults of our country, warrants a return to the "spirit of '63".

Politics in the union: from an Old Etonian president to a hotch-potch of Trots

Old Etonians are much in the news these days and even some Tories think it monstrous that they predominate in the coalition government. But there is, I believe, only one trade union or professional association that has had an Old Etonian as its president, and that is the National Union of Teachers.

G.C.T. Giles was its president in 1944-45. He had been a King's Scholar at Eton, but although it was before my time I'm sure he did not become president because he was an Old Etonian. The NUT is not, after all, like the Conservative Party. Giles would have been elected because he was a Communist and a very able one, and the CP was very active within the NUT, as it was in a number of other major unions at that time.

In later years, during my time as an official, three other Communists were elected president – Max Morris, Jack Chambers and June Fisher – and I enjoyed good working relationships with each of them. At the time of my appointment as assistant secretary in 1955 none of them was on the executive, but they were when I sought to become general secretary in 1974. I have no doubt that Max Morris, in particular, was keen to stop me getting the post. Nevertheless, when I became general secretary, he and the other Communists were generally friendly and helpful to me, in spite of my known opposition to Communists and their fellow travellers within the student movement. I must also say that, unlike the ultra-leftists who are now more numerous on the NUT executive than the Communists ever were, the CP-ers were always much more realistic about what the union could and should attempt to do, and much more aware of the nature and potential of the union. They were not strike-happy would-be revolutionaries and, of course, they detested the Trotskyists. Max Morris was once quoted in the *TES* as saying: "The Trots were a force to be reckoned with – I wouldn't pass the time of day – I used to shit on them from a great height, from the platform using ridicule." (*TES,* 18/10/96)

The Communists today are a dying breed if not completely dead as a force within the NUT and most other unions, although in some unions former or near Communists are still active, the most significant of whom was the late Bob Crow, rightly seen as one of the few "big hitters" in today's trade union movement.

Before considering the situation that exists within the NUT today, it is important to look back to the time when I first joined the union's staff.

The NUT has never been affiliated to the Labour Party and did not join the TUC until 1970, but there was a time after the Second World War when a number of its members became very prominent in the Labour Party. In fact, there is probably no other union that has produced as many Labour ministers as the NUT, and certainly no other union which has produced two Speakers of the House of Commons – Horace King and George Thomas.

The union was particularly proud of Chuter Ede, the joint architect, together with R.A. Butler, of the 1944 Education Act. Chuter went on to become home secretary and leader of the House of Commons. Three NUT members became secretary of state for education – Michael Stewart, Ted Short and Estelle Morris. Michael Stewart also served as foreign secretary and George Thomas as secretary of state for Wales, and much later Jacqui Smith became home secretary. In addition, in successive Parliaments an appreciable number of NUT members were elected as Labour MPs – at one point as many as 28 of them. Only two were elected as Conservative MPs and none as Liberals or Liberal Democrats.

For a long time the union had a scheme whereby it gave support to up to four MPs from each of the three main parties, who then acted as consultants on parliamentary affairs for the union. There were always a flood of Labour candidates who sought to do that work, but rarely any from the other two parties.

For years it was part of my job to handle relations with these MPs, and I enjoyed very friendly relationships with them. I also kept in touch with Tony Crosland when he became education secretary and arranged meetings for him at the annual conference with known Labour Party members who were delegates in order that he could discuss with them what he was seeking to do as minister.

I always regretted that Labour ministers did not have such meetings with Labour activists in order to get the benefit of the advice they could give on the way things were actually working out in schools. There were times in later years when I told ministers they should realise that they would not achieve what they were seeking to do without the support and advice of those on whom they were completely dependent to deliver what their policies and legislation called for. "You can't do it all from Whitehall" was my frequent message.

Regrettably, in time, relations between the union and successive education ministers deteriorated and before I left office they had ceased to address the union's annual conference, but the relationships never became as bad as they were with the Conservative education secretaries in the later years of the Thatcher government and particularly in the period of the 1985-86 dispute leading to the abolition of the Burnham Committee (the body which negotiated teachers' salaries). That was in stark contrast to the time not long after I became an official when Ronnie Gould was invited by David Eccles, the then education minister, to have lunch with him at his home. Ronnie asked me to go with him and Eccles agreed. We had a very enjoyable and constructive discussion with Eccles and he was at pains to tell us that he felt very frustrated that, having succeeded in getting cabinet support for increased funds for education, he had no real say in how those funds should be spent.

We complimented Eccles on his success in getting the funds but explained that it was in the nature of our education system that it was the local education authorities which were responsible for allocating the funds. How unlike the home life of our own dear education secretary today! Also how unlike the letter which I received from Sir Edward Boyle after he had retired from the cabinet in which he had served as probably the Tories' best, and certainly most liberal, education minister. During his time in office we had carried out our national survey of school conditions, and in his letter he thanked me and the union for the help that the survey had given him when seeking more funds for education, and hoped that we would keep in touch. I could not imagine for one moment Michael Gove ever writing such a letter.

That is not to suggest, however, that there have been no times when Conservatives have been active or influential within the union. When I first became an official the treasurer of the union was a Conservative who had been president and another prominent Conservative became president later. There was also at least one Liberal president and a number of others who had no particular political allegiance. At local association and county level in a number of areas, and especially in small towns and the countryside, there would have been officers with Conservative affiliations. It was undoubtedly a source of the union's influence and success in a number of disputes with government and individual local authorities that many members were prepared to put their loyalty to the union before their loyalty to the party they supported, and I am sure that has happened also on a number of occasions under Labour as well as Conservative governments.

What is almost certainly true is that in the union's membership as a whole, and possibly in the teaching profession as a whole, there has been something of a shift to the left, or to independence of any party, but not to the ultra-left which now enjoys a representation on the executive of the NUT which in no way reflects the views and political allegiance of the large majority of NUT members.

Among the groups and organisations that now seek to win the support of NUT members are the Socialist Party Teachers, Socialist Worker, Socialist Resistance, the Campaign for a Democratic and Fighting Union, and the Socialist Teachers Alliance. In the last two years another group has emerged which seeks to outflank the ultra-left by being even further left. It's called LANAC (Local Associations National Action Campaign) and by inviting NUT local associations to join has all the marks of what Militant Tendency tried to do within the Labour Party.

To lump this collection all together as a "bunch of Trots" would suggest a degree of cohesion which they do not possess, or a link with Trotsky which is somewhat tenuous. They are not like the Communists of my time who were disciplined and had a common party line. The far left in the NUT is a hotch-potch of different factions and organisations, some of which come together under the banner of the Socialist Teachers Alliance, but which does not include the supporters of the Socialist

Party Teachers faction and LANAC. The other main group on the executive is what used to be called the Broad Left and is now called Broadly Speaking. It enjoyed a majority on the executive until a few years ago and is seeking to regain it, but it lost three seats in the 2014 executive elections, whereas LANAC gained three seats.

These changes have led to something of a realignment within the executive, for LANAC and the Socialist Party Teachers faction can now be regarded as the hard left, and at the 2014 annual conference they sought to commit the union to bigger strike action than that proposed by what (for purposes of distinction) I will call the ultra-left. Broadly Speaking also supported more limited strike action, and together with the ultra-left succeeded in securing a substantial majority against the hard left in the conference. Although they were prepared to suggest more limited strike action, they were also prepared to acknowledge and tell the conference that in various parts of the country members were reluctant to take strike action on the scale urged by the hard left. It remains to be seen whether the ultra-left will be willing for the alliance with Broadly Speaking to continue or decide that it does not want to be outflanked by the hard left. And it remains true that one thing the ultra-left and the hard left have in common is that, with the possible exception of one or two ultra-left executive members, both factions are not Labour, and certainly not Conservative or Lib Dem. It also remains true that the very low level of participation by members in the elections for the union's officers and executive, to which I refer later, suggests either a degree of indifference or inactivity on the part of a very large section of the membership which is not good for the health of the organisation.

I'm glad that throughout my time as general secretary I never had to work with an executive of the present kind; nor did my successor, Doug McAvoy. But over the years since then the complexion of the national executive began to change. Gone were days when "Rank and File", the forerunners of the present-day hotch-potch, were not much more than a fairly noisy irritant on the floor of the annual conference hall with hardly any representation on the executive.

This is how Neil Kinnock, the former Labour leader, described the situation nearly 20 years ago in a statement to the *TES:*

> The great majority of the NUT are professional, committed, hard-working classroom teachers. Those who are activists are often what you would call social democrats who are extremely serious about their teaching commitment and very political in their attitude towards the NUT.
>
> But there is also the so-called Hard Left who, as far as I could see, did not give a damn about teaching or education and even less of a damn about their personal appearance or their responsibilities. They were yappers and because they did not do anything else with their lives – didn't go to football or concerts or any normal things – they were pretty well organised.

At the time when Neil said that, there were very few members of the "hard left" on the national executive and the national conference was not faced with the kind of agenda it faces nowadays. Incidentally, I guess they would prefer to be called the ultra-left. "Hard left" isn't too good for the image when trying to win support in places like Buckinghamshire and Wokingham.

The move leftward which has occurred among teachers, but which should not be exaggerated, has been generated first by disappointment and disenchantment with some of the things that the Blair government did, and now by the contempt and hostility that Michael Gove evokes, coupled with the growing pressures which many teachers are now experiencing in their daily work.

With the anger that is felt about Gove and his policies and statements, and some teachers feeling that things may not get much better under Labour, it is not surprising that the general mood of the profession assists, and is exploited by, the ultra-left in its efforts to win support within the union (they don't bother with the other school teachers' unions) but in my view it does not, and will not, lead the bulk of NUT members to vote for any of the utterly minuscule left-wing political parties which remain insignificant in the political life of the country.

There are some parts of the country where there is little evidence of ultra-left activity, where members don't need to deal with their propaganda and their efforts to commit the union to their latest proposals for action. It does not mean, however, that there are not some associations in those areas where members of one or other of the ultra-left factions will seek to get support for their candidates and their resolutions and the ordinary member is not aware of what they are up to. The list of nominations of election candidates and the conference agenda show where they succeed.

At the union's annual conference there is no mistaking the presence of the ultra-left. As delegates arrive at the conference hall they have to pass through an avenue of leafleteers and the messages of the literature they thrust into the delegates' hands are clear: "Vote for a National Strike", "No to Cover", "Stop the Spread of War", "We Don't Have to Pay for Their Crisis", "Organise for Resistance", "Strengthen the Plan of Action", "Time to Fight on all Fronts". All part of the warm-up for the fiery oratory that their activists will deploy from the rostrum as the conference proceeds.

And at any march or rally the union might organise they will bring placards galore which, when seen on TV, give the impression of support for action which is not borne out by members' attendance at union meetings or their voting in ballots for action or for the election of the union's officers and executive.

Before the 2010 general election, Mark Serwotka, general secretary of the Public and Commercial Services Union and the hero of the ultra-left, addressed the union's annual conference. His advice to the union's members was not to vote either for the Labour, Lib-Dem or Tory parties. He got a standing ovation led by his friends on the executive, but I'll wager his advice was totally ignored by most NUT members. At the 2013 conference he was back again and got another standing ovation when he urged the union to join with others in promoting a general strike or "national co-ordinated action". The NUT's delegates at the following TUC congress voted to support consideration of a general strike. That lunatic idea has sunk without trace but it was no credit to the conference delegates that while Serwotka got his standing ovation they listened in virtual silence when a delegate of the Broad Left had the guts to spell out the realities the union needs to face.

It is fortunate for education and the union that at local and county level the organisation continues to do its work effectively and its membership still grows. But, in my view, it is not wise to say, as some of my NUT friends do when they refer to what happens at the annual conference, "Well, that's just conference", as if it is some annual aberration by the seaside to be dismissed as of no consequence. That is unwise because while there are times when debates are very impressive (and too often ignored by the media) the overall image conveyed by the conference is not one that is likely to win the support of those sections of the public that the union needs.

The annual conference is the main union activity to receive regular and substantial media coverage, and as such it should truly reflect the views and aspirations and aims of the majority of its members.

The same should apply to the composition of the executive and the officers of the union. The union claims a membership of around 330,000. In the 2013 elections for the union's officers only 31,436 voted (10.2%). The candidate for treasurer was from the CDFU (Campaign for a Democratic and Fighting Union) and he was returned unopposed. Of the candidates for the posts of senior and junior vice-president, two were from the ultra-left, one from the hard left, and two were from the broad left. What is of particular interest is the identity of the associations which nominated the ultra-left and hard left candidates.

The participation in the election for the union executive is hardly more encouraging: whereas 22 candidates were involved in elections, another 19 were returned unopposed, and the level of participation in the 2014 elections was rarely more than 10%, and in only one case did it exceed 20%.

I appreciate there are times when local loyalties can play a part, and that sometimes teachers can turn radical when they see affluence at work, but I doubt if it can be seriously suggested that the NUT members in the following areas were aware of the political allegiances of the three far-left candidates who were nominated by their associations, along with others, for the officer posts. The areas, which can hardly be described as areas of deprivation or bastions of the working-class movement, were: Bedfordshire, Bromley, Buckinghamshire, Cambridgeshire, Cheshire West, Devon, Eastbourne, Fareham and Gosport, Folkestone, Hertfordshire, Ipswich, Kingston-upon-Thames, Lewes, Leicestershire, Merton, Norfolk, Warwickshire, Wokingham and Worcestershire. Should I have got it wrong, and union members in those areas were fully aware of the backing of the far-left which was being given in their areas, I've no doubt I will hear from them.

The election addresses the candidates circulate do not dwell on their political allegiances. It may be argued that members do not need to know the political allegiances of those who are to represent them, but when the decisions of the executive are determined by factions with political aims and views members ought to know what they are voting for.

It is surely just as important not only that members should exercise their right to vote but also that they should attend association meetings when nominations are discussed and the policies and future activities and calls upon members are considered. The same should surely apply to the composition of the national executive. But what happens nowadays is hardly reassuring. I realise it might seem presumptuous for a retired old codger to make such suggestions, and I appreciate the enormous professional pressures most union members are under nowadays. But as someone who was deeply grateful to be made an honorary life member of the union I feel sure that most of its members care at least as much about the future of the union as I do, and that they will want to see it go on to achieve even greater things than I have recalled from my time as one of its officials.

On another aspect of the "who speaks for the members?" issue, I would suggest that it is equally a matter for concern that so many candidates have in recent years been returned unopposed to the national executive. And the number of members who vote in the elections for officers and executive is deplorably low. In spite of all the pressures with which they now have to contend – and I realise that they are much greater than they were in my time as general secretary – it is surely in the members' interest that they recognise the relevance of the union to their future and that of their profession, and that those who take decisions on the union's future activities, its calls upon them and the views expressed in their name, do truly represent the views and feelings of the majority of its members and not those of tiny, yet very active, minorities.

There are undoubtedly things happening in education today which anger many teachers and may affect their futures, and there could well be worse to come, but I would suggest the union will be in a much stronger position to deal with them if it can involve and represent its members in the way it did for many years. In my opinion it needs to explore and utilise every way possible to engage that large majority of its members who at present do not attend union meetings, vote in the union's elections or respond to its ballots. Of course those of the ultra-left are unremitting in their efforts to win support for their cause(s) because that is what zealots do. But that is no reason for others to leave the pitch to them. I have no doubt that those of the moderate majority need the union as much as the union needs them, but they have to show they really care about it too.

I do apologise to those of my readers who are not greatly interested in the life or future of the NUT (though I hope some of you will be); but there are times when certain things need to be said, and I did say this book would be about my opinions as well as my memories.

To strike or not to strike –
is that really the question?

"Fred Jarvis, I remember you. You're the man who led the teachers' strikes when I was at school," said the youthful John Bercow, Speaker of the House of Commons, when I gave my name on asking a question following the memorial lecture for my dear friend Jack Ashley, at the Speaker's House.

So that's why Mr Speaker remembers me. I have organised what a prime minister (Harold Macmillan) said was "the biggest educational effort and the biggest combined effort to secure educational advance in the country in all our history". I devised and directed this country's first national education and careers exhibition, promoted a survey revealing the condition of the nation's schools, organised a major, star-studded conference on popular culture, and have done quite a number of other things, but it was because of the strikes that the Speaker, and maybe a few other people too, remember me.

Of course that is hardly surprising. Most of the media in this country have little interest in, or speak up for, good and useful events, but strikes affect families and communities, and in the case of teachers' strikes, primarily children and students like the young John Bercow, and the bigger the strike, the greater the number affected. And in my time as general secretary, NUT members participated in the biggest strike action yet staged by teachers in this country, and the media coverage of it was greater than at any time before or since.

Needless to say, teachers and other trade unionists do not like strike action, and their representatives and officials of their unions do not "lead" them in order to be remembered by the Speaker or anybody else. They do it, or rather should do, in order to achieve an objective which they have come to feel cannot be achieved by any other means, or when all other means have failed. If members of the public remember one's role it will invariably result from what they saw on TV, heard on the radio, or read in the press, and in the case of teachers that will relate principally to the strikes of 1985-86.

There are doubtless those in the NUT today who favour strike action on a range of issues, and who argue that it is only by resorting to strikes that teachers will win public support and force a government or their employers to concede their demands. It's not so long since the *TES* magazine published a feature with the theme "Let's go back to where we once belonged" (*TES*, 7/1/2011), in which while some of the teachers interviewed said teacher activism was in decline others were quoted as calling for the militant action that they believed to be the most effective way of meeting their professional needs. But is it, and is striking really "where we once belonged"?

If one is to look back to where we once belonged, it is as well that we should remember what has actually happened since those days in the early post-war years when the first stirrings of teacher activism occurred. The first serious attempt at action was over a proposal by the Tory government in the late '50s to impose an increase in teachers' pension contributions. It did not take the form of strike action, but refusal to collect National Savings money or to supervise pupils taking school meals. It nevertheless was a sufficiently powerful expression of teachers' anger over the government's intention that it led to an appreciably bigger pay increase than teachers had had previously. The widespread media coverage of the teachers' action had a salutary affect on the government and the employers.

The next upsurge of action arose in 1969, when growing hardship and dissatisfaction over pay had led the union to seek an interim pay increase before a two-year settlement had been completed. Teachers' anger increased when the employers and the government refused to consider any interim review and suggested possible referral to the Prices and Incomes Board, arguing that it was seeking to limit public sector pay increases to 3.5%. When it emerged that other groups were securing bigger increases (15% in the case of BOAC airline pilots), the determination to take action increased, fired now by resentment of unfair treatment and evidence of public support for the teachers' claim. That led at the end of 1969 to action by the union on an unprecedented scale. One-day and half-day strikes in many parts of the country and then spread over two months were a source of continuing media coverage. That action was followed by a two-week strike in one area to be followed in the new year by unlimited strike action in all areas and a national day of protest. Throughout the whole of this period there were numerous demonstrations, various events and meetings with parents around the country. More than three million leaflets were distributed and over 80,000 posters used, and for the first time the union took paid advertising space in the national newspapers. In addition, a film, *A Fair Day's Work,* was made and widely used.

In addition to the strike action by the union, the teachers' unions were unanimous in the teachers' panel of Burnham in pressing for the interim claim. They rejected offers by the employers to move from their original position by making offers of a £50 and then a £90 interim increase. Finally, on the day of national protest, when the Burnham Committee met they made an offer of a £120 interim increase which the teachers accepted. In all, some 150,000 NUT members had taken part in the union's action.

The next, and by far the most significant, pay increase for teachers came without any threat of or decision to take strike action – the Houghton award. The inquiry into teachers' salaries which was conducted by the committee chaired by Douglas Houghton was concluded within the framework of the "social contract" agreed between the Labour government and the TUC. While that agreement was aimed at securing a form of incomes policy, teachers were rightly given special consideration. Evidence from the union, greatly assisted by the trade union research unit at Ruskin College, had exposed the shocking extent to which teachers' pay had fallen behind that of other comparable workers in both the public and private sectors and had prompted the government to recognise the need to do something drastic about the inadequacy of teachers' salaries. That, together with the submission of other unions, influenced Houghton to award the biggest increase in teachers' pay that has been received by the profession, and which caused many teachers to tell of what they had been able to do with their "Houghton money".

It was no fault of Houghton or the Wilson government that the substantial gains from the award came to be undermined in the years that followed, due to the world-wide oil crisis and the horrendous rise in the rate of inflation which it caused.

Inevitably, as the time for the next general election approached, the unions in most parts of the public sector were seeking to recover the position of their members following the damage inflicted on them by the massive rise in inflation. It was against that background that the union attempted to restore the pay relativities that had been given to teachers by Houghton. During the course of those 1979 negotiations in the Burnham committee, the Callaghan government had set up the Clegg commission on comparability and the teachers' panel in the Burnham Committee submitted a claim for increases of the order of 30% (the amount needed to restore the Houghton levels).

It had been expected that the general election would be held in the autumn of 1979 and that, in spite of the problems caused by the world oil crisis,

Labour might win. The response of the employers to the teachers' claim in Burnham was unhelpful, no doubt fearful that the country might be facing a "winter of discontent". There was therefore a proposal to operate a form of work to rule to create pressure on the local authorities. Since the school caretakers were also taking action, the situation in many schools was becoming difficult.

The negotiations stretched over the period from January to May 1979. The key issues were the level of salary increases from 1st April 1979, the staging of subsequent increases in the light of government policy and whether teachers' pay should be referred to the standing commission on comparability.

The employers, with the support of the education secretary, Shirley Williams, had been prepared to agree a 9% increase from 1st April 1979, and reference of the claim to the standing commission, but the staging of such subsequent increases was on less favourable terms than for other public sector groups and the inclusion of Houghton in any terms of reference to the standing commission remained a stumbling block.

Very regrettably, Labour lost the election and within days Mark Carlisle, the new Tory education secretary, asked me to see him. I knew Mark from NUS days. He was a liberal-minded Tory, not likely to last long in a Thatcher administration (and he did not). He asked me what I thought he should do to deal with the impasse. I said I would say to him what I had said to Shirley Williams, namely that we would be prepared to go to Clegg if Houghton was included in the terms of reference. Although it had been expected that Thatcher would lose no time in abolishing Clegg, she did not do so. The Burnham Committee reached agreement on 21st May on a 9% pay increase from April 1979, reference of the claim to the standing commission with the subsequent increase being paid in two equal halves from 1st January and 1st September 1980, and terms of reference which included Houghton. It was not long before it was agreed that our case would go to Clegg, and I thought it saddening and bizarre that we were able to secure something from Mark Carlisle that we could not get from the government that had set up Clegg.

The Clegg commission's consideration of teachers' pay became one of the most complicated and contentious set of pay negotiations faced by the union. The commission's first report at the end of 1979 clearly validated the union's claim for the restoration of Houghton and set alarm bells ringing all over Whitehall. The commission subsequently tried to reduce significantly the pay increases for teachers. They and the government tried desperately to exploit an essentially technical error in their second report, which did not alter the fundamental position, to reduce the pay increases. Although that came too late to stop the initially recommended increases, the employers and the government tried to claw the money back from the 1st April 1980 increase. That dispute went to independent arbitration which found in favour of the union and teachers. The union was able to show in its detailed evidence at the arbitration that the employers' and the government's assertions were not borne out by the evidence.

Compared with the 1978-79 pay scales prior to the Clegg reference, teachers' pay by September 1980 had increased by between 46% and 58% despite the best efforts of the employers, Clegg and the government to short-change teachers.

The salary dispute which occurred in 1985-86 led to the biggest and longest action by the union at any time in its history to date. It began after the year-long miners' strike which had ended in defeat for the miners, and it was being said that having beaten the miners, Mrs Thatcher would "have the teachers for breakfast". It did not turn out like that although it was followed by the government's destruction of the teachers' salary negotiating body, the Burnham Committee.

The dispute began in 1985 at a time when the union had a majority on the teachers' side of Burnham. It lost that majority in the course of the prolonged dispute by a decision of the secretary of state to change the number of representatives of the individual unions. At the outset of the protracted negotiations, however, the union had its majority and the claim with which the negotiation began was one by which the teacher panel sought to restore parity of the order enjoyed in the post-Houghton period.

The initial reaction of the employers' panel was hostile and led to the first steps in action by the union. As a result of sustained pressure by the union, the employers shifted their position while the secretary of state remained opposed to any move in the direction they favoured. Eventually both sides agreed to go to ACAS, which recommended an interim increase of 5.8%, which was bigger than any increase in the rest of the public sector. It was not, however, acceptable to the secretary of state. The situation became further complicated when talks were held about aspects of the salary structure and the wish of the secretary of state and the LEAs to alter teachers' conditions of service. It was in the course of these talks, and in the absence of an agreement to implement the decision of ACAS, that the union lost its majority on the teachers' panel. Nevertheless, the mood of the union's members was such that they were prepared to take further action not only in regard to salaries, but in respect of "no cover" and aspects of the examination system.

In all, the union conducted some 14 ballots of its members in respect of various forms of action and in regard to the proposed settlement, and in each of them very substantial majorities were secured. Undoubtedly the scale and duration of the action the union was taking played a major part in securing the interim agreement to pay the 5.5% increase and a decision by the secretary of state to make more funds available for the development of the GCSE. Because of those developments, most of the different forms of action were ended in the summer of 1986, but no further agreement was negotiated in Burnham. The secretary of state eventually imposed a settlement on terms appreciably higher than he had been willing to contemplate when the dispute began, but in spite of intense lobbying by the union in respect of his bill to abolish Burnham, the bill was eventually passed by Parliament.

Throughout much of the prolonged dispute my colleague Doug McAvoy, as acting general secretary following my hospitalisation (after a car accident), led the negotiations in Burnham and the talks on salary structure and conditions of service. In spite of the union losing its majority on the teachers' panel, he continued to lead for the teachers' side and did so with great skill and determination.

I returned to work before the end of the dispute and was then greatly occupied with addressing meetings of our members and handling the big and continuing coverage of the dispute in the media. I was the subject of a number of profiles in the press and a special *Panorama* programme. In that programme I was filmed at a West Ham home game, a rally in Portsmouth and, for some reason I could never fathom, down at the site of the Thames barrier. Maybe someone at the BBC had the idea the union might be going to unleash a deluge.

There have been occasions since my retirement when there have been disputes about teachers' pay and conditions of service, and in recent years about pensions. The abolition of the Burnham Committee and of teachers' negotiating rights have, of course, not ended teachers' dissatisfaction or their aspirations in respect of their pay, pensions and working conditions; but it does mean that teachers and their unions have to deal with a situation different from "the days where we once belonged". Instead of putting pressure on employers and government by traditional means, there is a review body to convince by argument and evidence. And beyond that body stands the government of the day, with the ultimate power to accept or reject any award the review body might wish to make.

Given that the members of the union and the other teachers' unions are engaged in a public service, ultimately public opinion has a considerable bearing on what they are paid and what resources they will secure to do their work. For that reason, when considering what forces are most likely to shape public opinion, it is not enough only to consider what strike action has achieved or might have achieved. There are other ways of influencing public opinion and that is why, in looking back to "where we once belonged" and forward to what should be done in future, it is important to recognise the value and influence of all the other things the union and its members and others have done, and are doing, which promote greater appreciation of the role and achievements of teachers and their schools and colleges, which demonstrate the value of education to each community, our society and to the economy, and what education can do for every child and young person and for their parents and all citizens.

The NUT has done a great deal in this respect over many years, and I hope I have shown the nature and quality of some of that. Our films, our exhibitions and conferences, our publications and surveys and guides, our rallies and marches, our meetings and co-operation with a host of organisations and especially with parents and governors, these have all played their part and, of course, at local level things like school and college open days have a valuable role too.

Other teacher and educational organisations also make their contribution, and events like the televising of the National Teaching Awards do a great deal to bring to a larger audience real insight into the quality and achievements of the teaching profession. Even more profound in that respect is an event like the scene in the TV series *Educating Yorkshire* in which a young lad shows his classmates that he has finally overcome his stutter – a deeply moving episode which must have affected many viewers.

I would not for one moment suggest that teachers should not be able to take strike action to defend their jobs and conditions of service, improve their pay and pensions, or deny that there are times when strike action has secured improvements in those fields, sometimes remarkably so, as for example in the action to secure the interim increase in 1969-70. But what I do contend is that all the other activities I have mentioned have had at least as much effect, on occasion, as strike action and that it is essential for the union and the other teacher organisations to give even more attention to such measures than hitherto, for times have changed and public attitudes can change too.

This means, inevitably, considering what might be done instead of taking strike action when there is a major grievance or claim that has to be pressed and opposition from a government to be overcome. I believe consideration should be given to asking union members, instead of striking and losing pay, to contribute the money that would have cost to building up a substantial fund to promote their cause by all means open to them, particularly using press advertising and hoardings, but, equally important, exploring all the ways in which social media can be used to influence public opinion, and especially to put the case to parents.

I think that sort of approach would be preferable to having parents appearing on television condemning teachers for interrupting their children's education and also, in many cases, causing them family difficulties and having to spend money on child care.

It also has to be recognised that in the time of austerity which the country is now undergoing, and will continue to suffer for years to come, there are other sections of the public who are experiencing hardship and setbacks at least as serious as those being suffered by teachers, and that also may have an effect on their willingness to support teachers on pay and pensions.

I think it is also necessary for members of the NUT to consider seriously what proposals are made at the annual conference which, far more frequently than ever happened in my time with the union, call for strike action to be taken or considered not only in regard to pay and pensions, but on other issues as well.

Early in 2013 I attended an international teacher conference at Congress House organised by the union and concerned with relations with the OECD. At that conference Randi Weingarten, president of the American Federation of Teachers (AFT), made a speech in which she said: "We have to find new

ways to win support, for the old ways have failed."
I believe teacher organisations (and their members) should consider that message, for their problems are not different from those of their American colleagues, though they may face opposition somewhat less vicious than their American counterparts. The AFT is certainly acting on Randi's advice, for it has launched a major new campaign on the theme "Reclaiming the Promise for Public Education". The emphasis in the union's campaign is for its members to reach out into their communities, to work with parents and others with a stake in education, and pursue a range of activities that show the importance of education and the work of teachers to the future well-being of every child and to the nation's economy and to American society.

I argue in the next section of this book the urgent need to create a single union for all teachers, but it may take time to create that even when the idea is accepted, so in the meantime I would hope that these ideas could be considered.

Teachers United

Not long after I had made my last speech at the Trades Union Congress, in September 1989, I received a letter from Lord Houghton. Those readers who are able to recall the war-torn years of 1939-45 may remember Douglas Houghton as one of the country's most popular broadcasters. His weekly programme, *Can I help you?* gave advice to listeners on a whole range of problems, for which many of us were very grateful. But to the teaching profession of today Douglas was even more helpful. As I have already indicated, his pay review of 1974 resulted in teachers getting the biggest salary increase they have ever had. He could rightly be said to be the Patron Saint of the profession.

To receive a letter from him would at any time be a pleasure, but in this case especially so for he was writing about an issue which I believe to be of great importance to teachers and education. In my speech to the congress I had said: "In the case of teachers, over the years of disunity, thousands of pounds which could have been better spent servicing members have been spent on competing for them."

Since the last congress certain mergers had happened and others were contemplated. "But, in some fields nothing has happened. Ours, regrettably, is one of them. Yet with the growing threat to public education and teachers' jobs and rights, in no area is unity more desperately needed. To achieve that unity we must start with the two main unions – the NUT and the NASUWT. Whatever differences there may have been between us in the past, no matter how many difficulties have to be overcome, our two unions have far more in common than differences, and far more to gain by working together than by standing apart."

In his letter, Lord Houghton congratulated me on my speech and said: "Your plea for unity, although it fell on deaf ears, is the most important thing in the trade union organisation of the teaching profession. It is the disunity which had led to the break-up of the system of joint negotiations on teachers' pay. [Kenneth] Baker would never have been able to do what he did had the teachers' unions worked together."

Sadly, Douglas Houghton was right. My plea for unity fell on deaf ears – outside the ranks of the NUT. But that was nearly 30 years ago, and in the meantime a good deal has happened to make the creation of one united teachers' union a real possibility. Certainly the recent developments in education and other things that might happen are making it even more important that a serious effort be made by all the interests concerned to take the major step which would benefit not only all their members but, even more importantly, the future of education in this country.

Although I no longer have a role in the trade union movement, I am an honorary life member of the NUT and might be said to be partisan. But I have frequently declared my support for the creation of a single union, knowing that the NUT is prepared to give up our separate existence to create a united body. I return to the subject now with an even greater sense of urgency, but also with a feeling of encouragement from developments that have occurred in recent years and the extent to which relationships between the different teacher unions have changed.

Most notably, it is only when one recalls the bitter conflicts between the NUT and the NASUWT which took place during my early years at Hamilton House that it is possible to appreciate the major change in their relationship which has taken place. In 2013 they made their historic agreement to act together in what they called "an unprecedented joint campaign" on a series of issues.

One particular source of encouragement is that, clearly, the vast majority of teachers do not have to be persuaded of the need to join a union. According to one recent survey, 97% of them are members of a union. That makes them one of the most highly unionised groups in any sector of the economy. At present they choose to join one of several competing organisations. But supposing there were no organisations and they wanted to create one? What would its main characteristics be?

Would it be open only to men, or only to women? Would it be one which insisted that men should be paid more than women doing the same job, or vice versa? Would it seek to recruit only teachers with particular levels of responsibility or who taught particular subjects? Would it be open only to those who taught in one type of school as opposed to another? Would it want to be affiliated to the TUC, or be against such affiliation? Prepared for or against strike action?

I guess there might be other political distinguishing characteristics but those I have listed all used to be felt to have influenced the membership of one or other of the present major teachers' unions. But today they are not. Issues that until not long ago were a source of division have gone and would certainly not feature in the aims and objectives of a united teachers' union.

Moreover, I would suggest that more and more teachers wonder now what are the differences between the organisations that are sufficiently important to warrant separation and competition. If there are teachers who wonder, there are certainly many members of the public who wonder. They have no idea why there is separation. To them they are all teachers – "the teachers" – just as the doctors are all "the doctors".

And if they, or teachers for that matter, listen to what the various trade union leaders say, they find that more and more they are expressing the same criticisms of government policy and the damage that is being done to the education system and the pay, pensions and workload of their members.

They are not the only encouraging signs. Another is that all the main teachers' unions are now affiliated to the TUC and the National Association of Head Teachers has applied to join. And they are all in the same world organisation.

And should it be suggested that teachers are disunited in other countries, as if there is something inherent in teaching that favours disunity, there are, again, encouraging signs from abroad. The most significant example is that of Finland, now ranked the top-performing country in education. They once had 13 organisations; today there is one, the OAJ. Their example is being followed by Norway and Iceland. Similarly, in Canada there is one organisation in each of the individual provinces and one central body. In the USA, although an attempt to create a single organisation linking the National Education Association and the American Federation of Teachers failed, mergers between the two organisations have taken place in a number of states and are working successfully. In some other countries one union predominates over others, while the issues which divide teachers in France and Germany are not anything like the same as those that have divided ours.

Quite apart from the developments which have been helping to create better relations between the main organisations here, there are two other compelling reasons for taking the big step. The first is the situation that teachers are going to face with the increasing fragmentation of the education system, in the powers of individual schools as semi-autonomous institutions, the introduction of performance related pay and other developments affecting job security. All these point to the likelihood of a growing need for help for individual teachers at a time when facility time for union representatives is being reduced or eliminated.

Against this backdrop there is surely a need for unions to pool their resources to ensure support for their members. It is foolish to spend money on competing for members instead of providing better protection for them; millions of pounds have been spent in the past on competitive recruitment. It can only make sense now to recognise that unions are in a new ball game, confronted by thousands of autonomous institutions, umpteen "chains" and weakened local authorities – not forgetting what they have to contend with in the ever-widening activities of Ofsted.

I would not want to suggest that creating a single, united teacher organisation is going to be easy. Dealing with mergers never is, and in the case of teachers' organisations they are all well established and proud of their traditions and achievements, and they have a considerable number of employees whose interests have to be safeguarded. But at the end of the day the profession as a whole needs to consider what is best for the good of all teachers. It should also consider whether Jeremy Hunt, the health secretary, faced as he is by a united medical profession, would even for a minute think of abolishing the General Medical Council, as Michael Gove, not faced by a united teaching profession, treated teachers with contempt when he abolished the General Teaching Council.

Gove speaks now about the value of a College of Teachers because he sees that as what he believes would be a way of undermining the teachers' unions. He has already urged teachers to turn to ADEPT, an agency which does not really compare with the unions. So there should be no doubt why he would favour a disunited profession. One more compelling reason, therefore, why the teachers should now go forward to the creation of a body which will be not only a formidable opponent to a malicious minister, but also a force for good for education and the nation's children, as well as its teachers.

One further source of encouragement, as I see it, is the fact that following its 2013 annual conference the NUT convened a meeting of all interested parties to discuss the whole question of professional unity. I attended that meeting, and I was impressed by the spread and forward-looking nature of the discussions. The meeting was attended by the Association of Teachers and Lecturers (ATL), UCAC (the Welsh union) and received very positive messages from the NAHT and the ASCL. Regrettably the NASUWT was not represented, but a number of its members were present.

Had he lived, it would have been good for Douglas Houghton to know that, while there were those "deaf ears" in 1989, there are a lot who are listening today. And how good it would be if, having recalled what he had said about the price teachers paid when their negotiating machinery was destroyed, teachers determined to advance to the creation of Teachers United – a team that could take on all comers.

Addressing a 1984 rally on cuts in student grants.

Sergeant Fred Jarvis, Germany, 1947

"Fred's Red" – Anne Jarvis (above)
and with their children, Jacky and Robin (below)

Above: "Hammers" supporter Fred as TUC
president in 1987.

Below: his portrait of Bill Clinton.

Fred with Tory education minister Sir Edward Boyle
at a 1963 Campaign for Education meeting and
(below) with Labour leader Neil Kinnock.

Above: An NUT rally at the Arsenal stadium in Highbury in 1986.

Below: NUT members demanding fair pay for teachers.

One of Fred's candid shots – Michael Foot and
Neil Kinnock with (in the background)
Denis Healey and Jack Jones.

Below: Stephen Twigg is congratulated by a friend
after capturing Enfield Southgate from MIchael
Portillo in the 1997 general election.

The anticipation of new students arriving at
"Catz" – Fred's old college in Oxford –
and (below) students setting off to face their finals.

Eric Cantona   John Smith

Malcolm Arnold   Trevor Huddlestone

Two of the photos Fred took on his 1954 visit to the Soviet Union: postgraduate students in Leningrad and the May Day parade in Moscow.

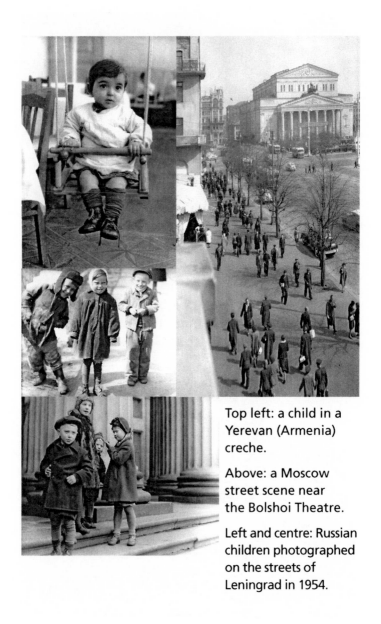

Top left: a child in a Yerevan (Armenia) creche.

Above: a Moscow street scene near the Bolshoi Theatre.

Left and centre: Russian children photographed on the streets of Leningrad in 1954.

Workers from GCHQ celebrate the end of the trade union ban – with a march through a cloudburst.

Below: Marching against the NHS cuts.

New York salutes the firefighters who died on 9/11.

Below: The Holocaust memorial in Berlin.

The collapse of Communism: a public meeting in Budapest in the run-up to Hungary's first free election in 1990.

Below: Demolishing the Berlin Wall.

Gordon Brown addressing the TUC and
(below) Tony Blair at his first party conference
after his election as Labour leader.

West Ham manager Harry Redknapp and (right)
Holly, a young Hammers supporter.

Below: A meeting with union leaders in the USSR
to discuss Chernobyl and (right) Swedish prime
minister Olof Palme with his son on his shoulders.

Five Labour Party leaders together: Jim Callaghan, Michael Foot, Tony Blair, Margaret Beckett and Neil Kinnock.

Below: MIkhail Gorbachev encounters Tony Benn at Fred's "Photo Opportunities" exhibition.

Left: Addressing a student conference at the UN Assembly building in New York. Right: Arriving at at 10 Downing Street for a TUC meeting with the prime minister. Below: Protesters at a TUC rally against the poll tax in Manchester.

Above: The mayor and *vignerons* of Ste Cécile toast the new vintage.

Below: The Kirov Ballet performing Romeo and Juliet in the Roman theatre at Orange.

Two of the thousands of pictures Fred has taken
in schools, colleges and universities at home and
abroad in the past 30 years.

Time in the TUC and Europe

Upon becoming general secretary of the union I was elected a member of the TUC general council, and served on it for 15 years. Prior to the union's affiliation to the TUC I went each year as an observer to the annual congress so I was already familiar with the scope and quality of the work of the congress. At its best, the congress really is the parliament of the world of work and in its debates a lot of the realities of the daily lives of millions of people are revealed. In recent years there has not been much of the vigorous debate that there used to be, partly because there are fewer divisions of opinion on big issues than there were in my time. A lot of good sense is spoken about life and working conditions in the public sector, whose members now constitute a much higher proportion of the TUC's membership given the decline of so much manufacturing industry.

The interest that I had found in so much of what was discussed at congress was amplified when I became involved in the work of the general council, especially, but not only, in those of its committees in which I was actively involved. I also became involved in quite a lot of European and international work because, with the UK's membership of the European Community, there was a great deal to do in the various committees and other bodies of the community.

While Margaret Thatcher had little time for consultation and none for partnership with the unions, at the European Community level there was a strong and equal role for unions alongside employers and government representatives.

A good example of what the partnership can mean was to be found in the creation of the EC's Centre for Vocational Education and Training (CEDEFOP). The representatives of the unions, the employers and the governments were all involved in the committee which drew up the basis for the establishment of the centre and on the board which was appointed to supervise its work. Two of the directors of the centre have been from the union. When it opened, the centre was situated in Berlin, and later transferred to Salonika. I was the TUC representative on the board from its establishment until I retired, and I greatly enjoyed the discussions and the development of realistic policies and advice it offered on the development of vocational education and training.

With my attendance at CEDEFOP meetings I went quite frequently to Berlin. That enabled me to get to East Berlin while the Berlin wall existed and then to be present in the city when the wall fell. It meant I got some very exciting pictures as the Germans started to attack the wall while Russian soldiers stood by. My CEDEFOP business also took me to Budapest at the time of the first elections to be held after the fall of the communist regime.

As well as my participation in European Community bodies as a TUC representative, I was also very actively involved in European teacher affairs on behalf of the union. Even before Britain joined the European Community the NUT played a very active part in European educational affairs as a result of its membership of the main teachers' international organisation, the WCOTP (World Confederation of Organisations of the Teaching Profession). That body had its own regional bodies, one of the most active of which was the European section, in which the NUT played a leading part. Another teachers' international organisation also had a European section and, after some disagreements, the two bodies joined together to form the ETUCE (European Trade Union Committee for Education), a body of which I became president before I retired.

Thus, with the work I was doing as a TUC representative on various EC committees and as an NUT representative in European conferences and committees for teachers, I had to spend quite a lot of time to-ing and fro-ing to Brussels and Berlin and other cities as well as also going to Australia and Oslo for meetings of the ICFTU (International Confederation of Free Trade Unions). But it was a field in which I was greatly interested – and still am.

It is very pleasing to note that some years after the ETUCE was created the two main teacher international bodies merged, and now have a very formidable and impressive organisation, called Education International, and that the teachers of a number of the former communist countries have joined them. I regard such developments as really encouraging to those who, like me, strongly favour a united teachers' body for this country. Another development which I believe should also be helpful to those who favour that cause is the fact that today all the main school teacher unions and the union for college and university lecturers (UCU) are members of the TUC, and that the National Association of Head Teachers has applied for membership.

I hope it was seen as a demonstration of the extent to which the composition of the TUC has broadened that I became the first representative of teachers to become president of the TUC. I know that there is the "Buggins turn" aspect of being elected to the presidency, but it is also an honour and a privilege to fill that post. In it one's main responsibility is to chair the general council and preside over the congress, to represent the TUC at union congresses in other countries and affiliated union conferences in the UK and at the Labour Party conference.

Occasionally a special body might be set up for a particular purpose, and in my case that resulted in an extremely interesting and important assignment. It arose from the disaster which occurred when there was a very serious accident at the nuclear plant at Chernobyl in the Ukraine. The work of the Nuclear Energy Review Body was concerned with one of the most serious problems facing all countries. The Chernobyl accident showed all too clearly that the serious consequences of a nuclear energy accident stretched well beyond the country in which the accident occurred.

The general council was quick to see the seriousness of the issue and was encouraged by the readiness of the Soviet trade unions to have discussions on the consequences of Chernobyl and what steps unions should take to open up serious international co-operation on and examination of the future use of nuclear energy.

It was a privilege to be involved in this very important project, and to be given the opportunity to visit a number of nuclear installations. In the UK we visited Dounreay and Greenock, then we visited a gigantic nuclear waste storage plant in Sweden, a nuclear plant in France, and most importantly of all, Chernobyl. I did not visit the Chernobyl plant because my wife Anne did not want me to go there, but I was involved in meetings with ministers in Kiev.

In addition to the programme of visits, I attended an intergovernmental conference at the headquarters of the International Atomic Energy Agency in Vienna, and after that an international trade union conference in Vienna which I was asked to chair.

I think that the work of the review body was one of the most important things in which I became involved during my 15 years on the general council. Of course it considered the very serious potential consequences of the use of nuclear energy, but it also led on to the need to consider the future use of all forms of energy and the ever growing and almost insatiable demands of the people of all countries for energy. There is a need for a far more serious and honest discussion of that matter than has yet been held in this country and internationally.

In addition to that very challenging responsibility, I had in the course of my time on the general council been a member of a number of key committees and chair of two – education and local government. Those two committees were of particular interest and importance to the NUT, and I gained much useful information and advice for the union from their deliberations. The same also applied to the part I played in a number of international conferences and trips to such countries as Yugoslavia, Australia, Norway and the USA.

Most helpful of all, of course, was the co-operation and help I received from the general secretary of the TUC and his colleagues, and from so many colleagues on the general council. They might be regarded in some media quarters as a bunch of barons, but for me they were a "band of brothers" (at least most of them). The camaraderie we shared then, often when confronting some very difficult decisions, was a great source of encouragement, and it continues among those of us who still gather from time to time for lunch at the Gay Hussar.

It wasn't a joyful year to be president of the TUC because 1987 saw Labour defeated in the general election. But there were still some enjoyable moments, like being given a standing ovation when I sang my version of "Mack the Knife" in a trade union setting at the congress of the AFL/CIO in Miami Beach; the very frank and friendly chat I had with Mick McGahey (vice-president of the NUM) at his birthday party at the NUM conference (Arthur Scargill was not there); the reception I held for all the press photographers at the congress; and the very warm reception I received when I put on the woolly West Ham hat and scarf with which I was presented at the end of the congress (they couldn't all have been Hammers supporters).

At the previous year's congress I had received a standing ovation after speaking on the 1985-86 pay dispute. There were 300 striking NUT members in the gallery and the ovation was really for them and their fellow strikers. It was a very moving occasion.

Now congress was warm in its reception of my presidential address, though I'm not sure that all the delegates would agree with some of the things I said (fortunately there's no vote on the address). Looking back at my address, made nearly 25 years ago, I am struck first by how much of what I said about the re-elected Thatcher government could be equally well said about the present Tory-led government. Secondly, I also feel that what I said about the role and tasks of our unions is still relevant to what they need to do today.

First, about government:

Mrs Thatcher says she wants to get government off the backs of the people; in fact her government has intervened more in the lives of working people than any previous administration. It is more intolerant, more authoritarian, more determined to weaken the protection offered to working people, more intent on undermining services which help ordinary people, and by its economic policies has exposed more people to unemployment and insecurity than any previous government. No-one can seriously suggest that we should stand by and let the government do that to working people, offering no criticism, no opposition and no alternative policies.

In its continuing attack on the trade unions the government pretends to be concerned for the rights of the individual. What it is actually doing is to elevate the rights of the individual above the rights of the majority and of union membership as a whole.

The real test of how much a government cares for the rights of the individual is what it is prepared to do to help the weak and the disadvantaged, the poor and the defenceless in our society. Judged by that criterion the record of this government, and its future intentions, show just how little it really cares about the individual.

True to its philosophy of giving more to those who already have most, of looking after those who are well endowed by wealth or ability and thus well able to look after themselves, catering, as always, for those whose first regard is for self and not for others, the government has step by step dismantled what has been built up over the years to protect and sustain the weaker members of our society – the disabled and the disadvantaged, the poor and the lowly paid.

The government's future intentions will take the process much further. The proposed break-up of the public education system will do nothing to help the least able children, or those from disadvantaged homes or even those of average ability.

And to the unions:

Not only do we have to face the challenge of the changing structure and patterns of employment, but we must recognise the changing attitudes and habits of working people too, changes which have clearly had their effect on political and voting loyalties.

But because there has been a vast and welcome extension of home ownership and car ownership; because many working people bought Telecom shares; because even more working people have credit cards, that does not mean they will have less need of the advice, assistance and protection, and collective strength that trade unionism provides.

On the contrary, the more rapid the changes in the pattern of employment become, the more job insecurity grows, the more employees face the arbitrary and often drastic decisions of employers, so the more vulnerable and anxious working people become about the commitments they have assumed and the improved standard of living they have achieved and seek to maintain. And the more then do they need the benefits of trade union membership.

None of us would claim trade unions are able to prevent all closures and redundancies, nor end all the uncertainty and hardships which changes in the economy and working practices can bring. But what we can claim and must assert is that those in membership of trade unions are less vulnerable to those dangers and anxieties than those who stand alone as individuals, waiting to be picked off one by one.

We have to realise the limits within which we can pursue the government's policies and activities. We cannot tackle every action or policy and we have to establish priorities. Moreover, we have to be sure that the policies we pursue are those most directly concerned with the general needs and expectations of our members, that they are seen to be relevant and will win the support of the bulk of our members. When we launch campaigns, we must ensure that we have the resources to carry them out and that we secure the participation of ordinary members in those campaigns.

After all that, how delightful it was to be black-balled by Margaret Thatcher. It related to my membership of the EC's economic and social committee. I had been nominated to be a TUC representative on this, the most important of the community's committees, toward the end of my time on the general council, but owing to a clash with union engagements I had not been able to get to any of the meetings. However, with the like-lihood that there would not be such clashes in future, I was nominated by the TUC for a further term. Some weeks later I received a letter from the Foreign Office thanking me warmly for the part I played in the economic and social committee but it was couched in such terms that it was clearly meant to be an end to my membership. I rang the TUC, which was shocked that for the first time one of its nominees for an EC body had not been accepted. Inquiries were made of the Foreign Office and it emerged that my nomination had gone up to the prime minister and she had personally rejected it. No doubt that example of Thatcher's vindictiveness was meant to convey her displeasure at the part I had played in the pay dispute of 1985-86. But being blackballed by Thatcher – can you do better than that?

Part 3: Extra-curricular activities

Did you say 'retirement'?

Over the years I guess I have had quite a few opponents – it goes with the territory – but I've had, to my knowledge, only one enemy: time. That is to say I've never had enough of it, I've wasted plenty of it, and have often failed to do or complete tasks I desperately wanted to carry out or had been required to do.

It was my fond hope that when I entered the state called "retirement" all that would change and I would no longer have my enemy to contend with. After all, in retirement you are "free" to choose what you will do with your time. Inasmuch as any of us are "free agents", at least up to a point, we can choose to drop or not start something which is proving too time-consuming – or simply not enjoyable. What I do find hard to understand is the friend who says he or she doesn't know what they will do when they retire. I find that specially puzzling if the friend lives in a city or a large town, and particularly if they live in or near London.

The city offers an enormous number of things to do, places to visit, events in which to participate or entertainments to enjoy. Of course, for some there are likely to be obstacles or difficulties, family commitments, health hazards, or a lack of cash; but for most that does not apply nor, theoretically at least, does lack of time. It is that which I find the problem. Although ageing is taking its toll, backaches and failing eyesight in particular creating difficulties, there are still so many things I want to do and mostly am able to do. Elsewhere in this book I talk of some of the things and places and people with whom I spend or have spent time. Here are a few more.

Theatre – an enormous variety to select from, and not all of it musicals. I go quite frequently and have only two complaints – first, in far too many of the theatres, in spite of refurbishments, the seating is damned uncomfortable, and of course prices often verge on the extortionate. My favourites include the National Theatre, the Milton Keynes Theatre and the Old Vic. And while I miss the satirical revues and the greats like Sid Field and Jackie Mason, thank heavens for Eddie Izzard, Bill Bailey and the superb gals of Fascinating Aida and save us from all those third-rate stand-ups who get vast sums for peddling rubbish.

Concerts and jazz – a remarkable range of opportunities. Favourites – Festival Hall, Cadogan Hall, the Royal Albert Hall and the Dankworths' "Stables". Not forgetting the Ukelele Orchestra of Great Britain.

Museums and Art Galleries – again superb opportunities but eyesight and backache making them less feasible than they used to be. But still I visit the Museum of London, the Courtauld, the National Gallery and Tate Britain.

Cinemas are plentiful and I much enjoy the Lumiere, London's most comfortable cinema, and the Curzon; but one can also get a good evening at the Community Cinema in Potters Bar. What is good about them is that you have a chance to catch up with films you missed the first time around.

There are also great opportunities for intellectual entertainment. I think Gresham College is a terrific venue for excellent lecture series, and it is completely free. As a Fellow of the Royal Society of Arts I frequently go to lectures and debates on a variety of topics; my only regret is that there is never enough time for questions and discussion with the audience. The University of the Third Age is a great example of social enterprise, and one of my old NUS chums, Ralph Blumenau, is one of its star lecturers.

When I am not sampling all these delights, I'm fortunate that my circle of friends has not been too diminished by the passage of time and departure of dear friends. The older you get the more you realise that friendship is the greatest treasure one can share. Forget possessions, trips and even books – it is the company of friends and the warmth of their friendship that matters most.

I guess reliving "times past" is an inescapable part of retirement, however active or inactive one might be, but I certainly enjoy the regular get-togethers with old friends and comrades from my days in the NUS and the TUC. It is hard to face the reduction in our numbers when one veteran follows another off the stage, but we still get great pleasure from swapping yarns and recalling past battles and triumphs. My TUC colleagues and I hope we will long continue to be able to lunch at the Gay

Hussar with its many reminders of the great days and personalities of the Labour and trade union movements.

What also matters more and more is the kindness of other people, the offer of a helping hand that is so quickly proffered in so many places. That, to me, is part of the essence of the good society. That's why I believe in collectivism, because that is what it is derived from. I don't care, however, for those politicians who talk about the Big Society but then pursue policies which are divisive and pitch citizen against citizen.

It is very saddening that as age advances one gets to attend more funerals and memorial events for beloved friends. So it is exhilarating when one has the opportunity to meet with and make new and younger friends and an enormous pleasure when one can be involved with young people. For nearly 20 years I was a member of the National Youth Theatre council, a terrific institution which brings great credit to this country and nurtures an enormous fund of talent which produces some of our greatest actors. It is equally exhilarating to get to the Schools Proms every year. As I say elsewhere, these proms and all the other activities promoted by Music for Youth are outstanding and unequalled anywhere else in the world.

New visions for education

Soon after my retirement from the NUT, Jack Straw, the then Labour shadow education secretary, invited me to join an advisory group he had set up to assist him in developing education policy. When Anne Taylor took over from Jack the group continued its work. Most of its members were professors of education or researchers and I really enjoyed working with them. In addition to offering advice to Anne, I suggested to my colleagues in the group that we ought to expose the backward-looking policies of the Tory education secretary of the day, John Patten. That led to a letter to the *Guardian* attacking Patten's new white paper *Choice and Diversity* (1992). The letter called for an alternative vision of education. We followed that with a booklet published by the Institute for Public Policy Research (IPPR) called *Education: a Different Vision – an Alternative White Paper.*

In the 1992 general election I ran a volunteer education unit for the Labour Party and a number of members of the group assisted in its work. Labour lost that election but the group continued to meet with the aim of advising the shadow education secretary. For the 1997 general election I was installed at the party's election HQ in

Millbank, assisting on educational issues and organising a bigger network than previously, with particular attention to getting Labour's education case across on phone-in programmes and in the media generally.

Following Labour's election victory I suggested to David Blunkett, the new education secretary, that the group should continue and that given the authority and experience of its membership it could give him some valuable assistance. David agreed to meet the group and we had what I believe both sides felt was a very useful and constructive discussion. Ted Wragg, the country's most popular educationist, had become the chairperson and, with leading figures in education among its membership, the group grew in size. During the Labour administration we prepared a series of papers on a number of issues, organised forums at the general elections, and a series of debates in co-operation with the *Guardian.*

Today, the New Vision Group has more than 100 members (and, uniquely, includes seven knights, four dames and a peer, all of whom have been recognised for their outstanding services to education). It was an enormous loss when Ted Wragg, our first chairperson, tragically died at all too early an age. He was succeeded by Tim Brighouse, another leading educationist who, as commissioner for London schools, led the highly successful London Challenge. He has now been joined as co-chair by Professor Geoff Whitty, who was director of the country's leading education centre, the Institute of Education of London University.

To act as convenor of the group has been, and continues to be, one of the most enjoyable of my activities in retirement. It is a privilege and a real pleasure to be able to work with so many colleagues who have done so much for the cause of education, and who can do so much for that cause in the difficult years that lie ahead.

I also greatly enjoyed working with Tim Brighouse when he was chief education officer for Birmingham, and created the exciting and forward-looking venture – the University of the First Age (UFA).

The UFA offers a range of transformative programmes that are interactive, fast-paced, with high challenge and high support to foster interdependent learning. Since its foundation in 1996 it has worked with over 750,000 young people and 6,000 adults in 50 regions and also worked with groups in Jamaica and Australia.

Tim invited me to become chairperson of the UFA board and I held that post for ten years. It was great to see how successful the UFA became and how the basic idea was taken up in other parts of the country. It was also very gratifying when David Blunkett, in one of his last decisions as education secretary, agreed to a grant for the development of the UFA.

My other retirement activities in the field of education have included spells as a governor of a primary school and a girls' comprehensive school in Barnet. They are both excellent schools and it was a privilege and a pleasure to be involved in their lives. I also served for several years as a trustee of the Trident Trust, one of the country's biggest providers of work experience for schools. Interestingly enough, two of my fellow trustees were (Tory) ministers in the coalition government. One of them, Lord Howe, is a minister in the Health Department. The other, Ed Vaizey, in the Arts and Sports Department, is the son of John Vaizey, who did so much to help the Independent Committee on Investment in Education which was set up by the union.

A cock-up at No 10

Not long after I had left Hamilton House I became involved in what has been one of the most stimulating (and I must confess most enjoyable) episodes in my retirement – what Prime Minister John Major's aide called "one of Downing Street's epic exchanges of correspondence".

The exchange lasted two years and began when I wrote to John Major in July 1991 posing a series of questions about statements he had made in his first speech on education after assuming the premiership. In the course of the exchanges, the prime minister gave a number of what I considered unsatisfactory and/or evasive replies. As the correspondence proceeded, it was reported in the *TES* and evoked comment in *The Times* and when it was concluded I published all the exchanges in a booklet entitled *Education and Mr Major*.

When they wrote their book *Too Close to Call*, John Major's principal aides, Sarah Hogg and Jonathan Hill, revealed the cock-up that had occurred at No 10 in the handling of the correspondence. At one stage the prime minister himself had apologised for the "sloppiness". Hogg and Hill explained that when my first letter had been received at No 10 it went to the political office when it should have gone to the private office, and had been dealt with by a junior member of staff who had sent a "bog-standard" reply, seemingly under the impression that I was a member of the Conservative Party.

Jonathan Hill is now a peer and Tory leader in the Lords. He was amused when I saw him in the House and told him how much I had enjoyed Sarah Hogg's footnote in the book which said, "If by any chance Fred Jarvis should read this, Jonathan says: please, please don't bother to write."

Further light was thrown on what had happened when *Private Eye* revealed that the minion who had handled the first stage of the correspondence exchange, one Stephen Yorke, had been sacked for his "sloppiness". Regardless of who deserved and who got the blame for the initial mishandling of the correspondence, it would have been good if John Major had acted on the advice I offered in the last paragraph of the final letter of the saga. I wrote: "You speak about 'common sense' values, but where is the common sense in persisting with policies that are divisive, that deliberately discriminate against large numbers of our children, and are largely irrelevant to their real educational needs? Where is the common sense in persisting with the application of 'market forces' as the main plank of your policy when even a right-wing think tank like the Institute of Economic Affairs is having second thoughts about such a policy and when the National Education Committee, which was given your 'blessing', is, according to press reports, about to challenge it? Where too is the common sense in further panic measures to promote 'opting out' when it clearly has so little support in the vast majority of schools? An ability to learn from one's mistakes is an important part of the educational process. I commend it to you."

Putting paid to Patten

John Major's education secretary at the time of the epic correspondence was the hapless (and hopeless) John Patten. I got involved with an episode in his career which he will surely regret.

Speaking at a fringe meeting at a Tory party conference, Patten had made a slanderous attack on my friend Tim Brighouse, who at the time was the chief education officer for Birmingham. When Tim learned of the attack he was naturally angry and concerned, and wondered what action he should take. I suggested that Patten's remarks were damaging enough to warrant legal action. Tim was uncertain about that, given the costs that might be involved, but I said I thought we could raise the funds for an action by appealing for donations from all those who knew of Tim's excellent work in Birmingham and Oxfordshire.

Tim finally agreed that we should organise an appeal, which a group of us did. We very quickly raised enough for an action against Patten and Tim engaged the services of the hugely skilled solicitor Geoffrey Bindman. The action was successful and Tim continued his excellent work in Birmingham, which was later followed by his outstandingly successful work on the London Challenge. Some time after the court settlement, John Patten resigned as education secretary. There were no reports of tears being shed.

Safe in the hands of the NHS

Recently I had a phone call from a friend, who had gone to join her daughter in Los Angeles following the death of her husband. She said she had returned to this country because she had found the cost of health care in the US unsupportable. That in the country which at the time of its last presidential election treated us to vox pop interviews on TV with ordinary Americans denouncing the idea of "socialised medicine" and predicting the disasters which Barack Obama's limited health reforms would inflict upon them and their country. No doubt some of those interviewed would have come from America's large lunatic fringe and the Mad Hatter's Tea Party which sees anti-statism as their only hope. But I believe my friend's inability to face the cost of health care reflects the experience of many Americans. Nevertheless, they would run a mile from the idea of a National Health Service like our own, such is their ignorance of what the NHS actually does for us, as well as the prejudice fomented by the powerful vested interests that want to maintain the status quo in health in the US.

I can understand why those powerful forces do what they do to protect their interests and profits. What is less understandable is the extent to which sections of the British media have been promoting a hue and cry against the NHS which could, and may be intended to, undermine public support for a service which remains Britain's outstanding social reform and of which even George Osborne, the Tory Chancellor of the Exchequer, has said "the NHS is the very embodiment of fairness in our society". Unquestionably, there have been a number of failings in parts of the NHS in certain parts of the country and they have been rightly condemned. But should they be allowed to promote a loss of confidence in the whole service and the basic principles on which it was founded? Each of us must answer that question in the light of personal experience. For what it's worth, I'll offer my view as someone who can be described as a "regular customer" of the NHS.

My experience of health care prior to the NHS was very limited. As a kid I had a short spell in Samson Street Hospital in West Ham, due to an attack of scarlet fever (remember that?) followed by a somewhat longer convalescence at a hospital in more distant Brentwood, which I revisited many years later following a severe nose bleed!

My first serious treatment under the NHS came well into my career with the NUT, and its outcome is something for which I have been profoundly grateful ever since. It came from an attack of gout which introduced me to the rigours of pain in no uncertain fashion, and which caused difficulties in my work for some time. As luck would have it a member of the NUT executive, Jack Chambers, hearing of this affliction, told me his daughter was a doctor at Guy's Hospital and that she could put me in touch with a colleague who was one of the country's leading gout specialists. Thus I became a patient of Mr Tom Gibson, who gave a great deal of attention to my case and to whom I am profoundly grateful for his skill and patience, the result of which is that I have not had another attack of gout in more than 30 years. Only those who have experienced the affliction will appreciate what a relief that has been.

My next spell with the NHS was longer and more complicated. It began with my being knocked down by a car as I was crossing a road, and suffering what was later described as a "bumper fracture". Unfortunately the fracture was not spotted at the A&E department at Barnet General Hospital and the doctor concerned said I could return home. Overnight my knee became very badly swollen and on return to the hospital the fracture was detected but, because of the swelling, the leg could not be put in plaster for some days. My immobility brought something worse – a pulmonary embolism that led to me being rushed to intensive care. Again, I had cause to be profoundly grateful to the medics who helped me overcome that setback.

Gradually the knee fracture responded to treatment and I could walk again but more trouble came with the onset of a prostate problem which led to a return to Guy's Hospital for an operation. All this contributed to what, if you were a Queen, you'd describe as one's *annus horribilis,* but it meant that I saw at first hand something of the pressures which hospital staff have to contend with in the course of their work. I wrote a full-page article about this for the *Guardian* to which I will return shortly.

Inevitably, I suppose, as happens to most of us, as we grow older the adversities of age take effect and with life expectancy increasing we experience more of them than our predecessors. In my case, the quadruple heart bypass I underwent some time after my retirement was about par for the course. It was done at the Heart Hospital, a splendid place that has been private and then returned to the public sector. The procedure was successful and although contemplated electric shock treatment for heart flutter was not proceeded with, one consequence of the medication I had for that condition was a series of severe nose bleeds which necessitated overnight stays in several hospitals, including the one in faraway Brentwood where I had been as a child, such being the pressures on A&E departments.

The hernia operation I had in 2012 was not due to advancing age; but the eyesight problem I now have to contend with is, at least in part, down to that. It means I have added to the tally of hospitals I have frequented an outstanding institution with an international reputation whose staff come from so many different countries that it feels as if one has come to the United Nations building. That aspect of its staffing is not by any means unique to Moorfields. What is striking about the hospitals I have frequented, and what is probably true of most NHS establishments, is the high proportion of staff who come from overseas. I can only think that those who rant so vehemently against the presence of immigrants in our country have little idea of the extent to which the NHS is dependent on other countries, and particularly "developing" ones, to meet the needs of its patients.

I've described these experiences at some length not because they are in any way out of the ordinary, but because I want to reiterate what I said in my *Guardian* article about the enormous pressures that those working in our hospitals have to contend with. The observations which I quote from the article are not those of an under-cover cameraman or journalist posing as a staffer, but of an actual patient. While much has undoubtedly improved or changed in the NHS since my "gout days" (for one thing, Barnet General is no longer a collection of hutted wards between which patients were sometimes moved on their beds in bad weather) my recent visits to hospitals have shown how most of the pressure continues and is inherent in the nature of hospital work, and is shared by GPs, district nurses and the paramedics from whose care I have often benefited, and all the support staff.

I am no expert on the management and manpower needs of the health service, but in the light of my recent experience and observations as a patient in a major teaching hospital and a general hospital, I believe that when the House of Commons public accounts committee insists that the health authorities must "control manpower" it either does not know or does not care what that implies as far as patient care is concerned. I believe it can only mean a failure to give patients all the care and attention they require and the substitution of financial for medical criteria in the treatment of the sick.

What determines the manpower needs of a hospital? Primarily the real and imagined needs of each and every patient. "Imagined" as well as real, because every patient before and after an operation or course of treatment is subject to a range of moods and anxieties which are peculiar to himself or herself, and which are almost as much in need of attention as the pains and physical consequences of treatment. Indeed, those moods and anxieties in many cases surely affect the potential success of the medical treatment itself. But in many cases they are quite unpredictable, both in their nature and intensity.

In any hospital much of the time of the doctors and nurses and ancillary staff is devoted to a set of routine tasks, and one of the most welcome features of hospital life nowadays is that aspects of the routine are less rigid and inconsiderate in terms of the patients than they used to be.

As a patient one can know little of the demands on the doctors and surgeons and their collaborators, simply because, in the day-to-day life in the ward, one sees much less of them than the sister, nurses, auxiliary nurses and domestic staff. And in the most crucial matter of all – where an operation is concerned – one is totally unaware of the enormous skills deployed by the surgeons and their supporting team, and the pressures they have to cope with, thanks to the vital skills of the anaesthetist.

But day-to-day life in the ward is a different matter. The pattern of the main routine is obvious – the dispensing of drugs; the observation and charting of pulse, temperature and blood pressure;

the feeding and cleaning of patients; the making of beds; the clearing up of messes; the recording of information and the answering of inquiries. That, however, is only one aspect of the manpower need which the politicians insist must be considered. Clearly, that need could be reduced – for that is what the demand for "control" really means – by performing at least some of those tasks less frequently and less thoroughly. But I doubt whether any of my fellow patients would have felt that that would have benefited them.

However, the routine tasks, important though they are, are only part of the pressures and demands on the ward staff. What can take up even more time are the needs of the individual patient to have his or her particular anxieties and problems dealt with. There can be no question of those demands being fitted into any routine; they can erupt at any time of the night or day, and they can be as different as one person is different from another.

In my observation, no member of the ward staff in the course of the inordinately long hours which most of them work, was ever at a loss for something to do. On the contrary, the almost invariable response to a call for help or attention was "Yes, I'll be with you just as soon as I can" – or, in cases of urgency, asking another nurse or an auxiliary nurse to take over the task in hand while the more urgent need was attended to. (If there are demarcation lines in the ward, they are not obvious to a patient.)

I see no way in which a hospital administration can control that aspect of its manpower needs, whatever any minister or House of Commons committee might say, unless it is by telling sisters and nurses and auxiliaries to do what they can in the time available and forget the rest.

Inescapably, any caring service, and especially the hospital service, is bound to be labour-intensive. And if the coalition government wants to persuade electors that the NHS is safe with it, then it has to face up to all the service needs, and all that the patients need, in terms of skilled and dedicated manpower.

And here, of course, one comes to the central issue. With over four million unemployed – including many health service workers and teachers who have already lost jobs, or who simply cannot get employment in the NHS or education service – Britain certainly does not lack the ability to meet the needs of labour-intensive services so far as manpower is concerned. Indeed, with the advance of technology reducing the manpower needs of so many branches of industry, what more satisfying way of providing employment could be found for many of the unemployed than by training them for jobs in caring services?

What is determining the satisfaction of the needs of the sick and the nation's children, and the needs of the old and disabled, is not the lack of available manpower but lack of the political will to provide the money to employ all those whom the health, education and other social services so urgently require to meet the needs of their clients.

No matter what those American voters might say about "socialised medicine" or those in this country who want to dismantle the NHS would seek to achieve, I would assert that while there have been times when I have been worried about my health (or have been annoyed about long waiting times) I have never been worried about getting the treatment I require or how I would find the money to pay for it. That certainly has not been a question of luck.

Footnote: Since I opened these reflections with reference to the prohibitive cost of health care in the US, I add this footnote to indicate my very limited experience of those costs. In 2008 I went to New York with the intention of taking pictures of American trade union action in the presidential election campaign. On the way to the venue where I was due to meet American union officials I tripped up a kerb, falling flat on my face, and was rushed to hospital where it was thought I might have broken my nose, contracted pneumonia and affected my heart. I was discharged after three nights and told that the hospital could not supply the four antibiotic tablets I would need to complete my treatment. I would have to get them from a chemist. I did – and they cost $64.

But what annoyed me even more was that I missed a great photo opportunity. I was on the 18th floor of the hospital and outside another structure was rising, and sitting on the girders were construction workers with their tools and lunch-boxes. Thinking this would give me a chance to do an update of that great, iconic pre-war picture of the same scene I looked for my camera – only to learn that my friends had taken it to their home for safe keeping. Hell!

The night I met Frank Sinatra

I guess it started with Muggsy, "it" being the thrill one gets when meeting a musician or artiste whose work you have listened to at concerts or on discs or the radio, or even danced to.

Muggsy Spanier and his New Orleans Jazz Band gave me my first experience of jazz. Until we moved to Wallasey during the war I had heard very little jazz, or for that matter most other kinds of music. When we lived in West Ham we had a gramophone and a very limited batch of records. It ranged from Gracie Fields and Sandy Powell to the Laughing Policeman and Broadway Melody, memories of which were rekindled when it featured in Gene Kelly's film *Singin' in the Rain.* Apart from those 78s I took in little music beyond occasional pieces on the radio. It was something of a revelation, therefore, when John Betts, the music teacher at Plaistow Sec (the secondary school I entered in 1935) introduced us to classical music with a series of gramophone recitals starting with Dvorak's unforgettable *New World Symphony.* But still no jazz, just some dance music we had at the school's Friday night "hops".

So a new world opened up for me when my school friend in Wallasey, Art Selling, invited me to hear his jazz collection. We had our fill of Armstrong and Ellington, Artie Shaw and Benny Goodman, Eddie Condon and Joe Venuti, but for me the greatest was Muggsy. There was, of course, no prospect in the war-time years of actually getting to see performances by any of these superb musicians, certainly not in England. But for me a chance came in 1951 when I went to the States as a delegate to the World Assembly of Youth at Cornell University.

When the assembly finished we were given the opportunity to go on a trip to various parts of the States, and I chose Chicago. Off we went by Greyhound bus to the Windy City and had a less than welcoming arrival. Our hosts had put us up in a YM and while we were all away from our dormitory taking showers to freshen up some enterprising character rifled our luggage and took all our cash. Upsetting, but then it was Chicago. That setback overcome by our hosts, I discovered that Muggsy Spanier and his band were in town and whooped with joy at the prospect of hearing him live at last. But even better was to follow. During the interval of their performance, I met the band's white trombonist, Ralph Hutchinson, in the loo. He turned out to be a Geordie and after chatting he offered to introduce me to Muggsy and "the boys". What luck, what a thrill, which was enhanced when Ralph gave me a photo of the band signed by Muggsy and all the boys. I always wondered how a Geordie could have landed a place in a New Orleans band, but never found out.

Later that week I heard Count Basie and his band at the Blue Note. Good though the evening was, it could not compare with meeting Muggsy.

After we were married and when our children were older, we all went to jazz sessions at New Merlin's Cave and in later years we went to Ronnie Scott's. What was great about Ronnie's (which I listed as my club in *Who's Who*) was the chance it gave to meet and chat with some of the greats in jazz, such as the outstanding saxophonist Ben Webster, and the magnificent Oscar Peterson. On another occasion, after hearing her at Ronnie Scott's, I had a chance to chat with a rather lonely Blossom Dearie at Pizza in the Park, in marked contrast to the time when, literally, I sat at the feet of the "oldies" in the legendary Preservation Hall in New Orleans.

For a number of years we went to Ronnie's for the Christmas performances of the incomparable George Melly and John Chilton's Feetwarmers. They were always hilarious occasions. Not so cheerful was the time when I heard George and the band perform in Berlin. Joining him at the bar during the interval I found George was miffed that the Berliners did not seem to share his sense of humour. Now there's a surprise.

Much nearer to home it used to be great, in addition to hearing him play locally, to often see and chat to Humphrey Lyttelton as he pushed his trolley round our local Waitrose. What a character, what a musician, and a staunch Labour supporter. How much we all miss him.

And what greater thrill could there be after playing so many of their CDs, than to see the wonderful Ella Fitzgerald at both Ronnie's and the Albert Hall, and to see Joan Baez many years after first playing her discs, still singing magnificently at the Festival Hall, and Barbara Dickson at the Stables (and in Potters Bar) and to chat with the seemingly ever-lasting Stéphane Grappelli at his various birthday and farewell performances at the Barbican.

None of these chance encounters added to or detracted from the great quality of their performances, but they do give a thrill and it is gratifying to find that they are also warm and kind as individuals.

In the field of classical music it is not usually possible to enjoy such chance encounters, so it has been a special pleasure to have met the great Yehudi Menuhin, our greatest conductor Sir Simon Rattle, and that rising star, Gustavo Dudamel. The occasions when I met them were quite different in character. I met Menuhin with NUT colleagues when we entertained him to lunch in preparation for the Chuter Ede lecture he had agreed to give for the union. He struck me as a most gentle, sensitive and very enlightened person blessed with a some-what domineering wife. Simon Rattle was an inspi-ration as he conducted more than 3,000 young musicians at the Birmingham Arena, described by the Guinness Book of Records as the world's biggest orchestra. He was dynamic and had great charm; I took many shots of him as he conducted and the resulting pictures provided a link when I met Gustavo Dudamel.

The brilliant young Venezuelan was at the Royal Festival Hall with the magnificent Simón Bolívar Orchestra. It was an extra concert put on to meet great public demand and Dudamel was not actually conducting but sitting in the audience. At the interval I spoke to him and having heard of his work with Simon Rattle I told him I had some pictures of Simon that he might like to see. Two days later I took them to the Festival Hall when Dudamel was rehearsing with the orchestra. He thought I was just showing him the pictures but when I said they were for him to keep he gave me a great hug and said, "I am so grateful. He has been like a father to me."

I imagine meeting ballet dancers is also difficult (unless you are a "stage door Johnny") but for me it did happen once while in Leningrad with a TUC delegation. We had been taken to the Mariinsky Theatre to see a performance by the Kirov Ballet. After the ballet we were taken backstage to meet the dancers (the host of our delegation was the president of their union) and it was a delight to meet and talk with them. Years later, I was able to see the company again in a vastly different setting when it was performing *Romeo and Juliet* in the Theatre Antique at Orange, the biggest of its kind in Europe. *Romeo and Juliet* is my favourite ballet: I must have seen it ten times by now, including one magnificent performance by Rudolf Nureyev (a fugitive from the Kirov) and Margot Fonteyn. What a joy it would have been to meet them after that show!

My two other chance encounters with great artists were yet again very different in character. The first of them verged on the bizarre. It happened at 10 Downing Street, the home and office of the prime minister, during Harold Wilson's premiership, and the occasion was a dinner for the prime minister of Fiji. My wife and I were among some 65 guests, and I guess I was there as the statutory trade union leader included on such occasions (at least by a Labour prime minister). In the general order of things I doubt that this dinner would be listed as a particularly important occasion, though it was enjoyable enough.

After the meal and the inevitable speeches we all adjourned to a lounge for drinks. I was sitting at the end of the lounge near to the door. As I sipped my drink the door opened and, to my astonishment, who should appear but Frank Sinatra accompanied by Barbara Marx, the widow of the great Groucho. I did not think he was likely to have any particular connection to Fiji (though doubtless his records would sell as well there as most other places), so I was bemused by his entrance. It looked as if the same applied to Frank, and as nobody else approached him I went over and said how great it was to see him at No 10. As he seemed to have no idea what kind of occasion it was, I tried to explain as best I could without giving the impression that this was a kind of Third Division match. Frank thanked me and was then approached by officialdom, but before it took over I told him how greatly I enjoyed his performances and could I please have his autograph. Without hesitation he agreed and, as to the manner born of millions of such occasions, he signed my table plan "Hi kids. Love Frank Sinatra". Years later I bumped into an old Oxford chum, Gerald Kaufman (now Sir Gerald) who had been a member of the Wilson entourage at No 10. I said it had been great to meet Sinatra at No 10 and

I had wondered how he came to be there. He replied: "When I wanted to meet somebody I liked, I got Harold to invite them to No 10. That's how I got to meet Ginger Rogers."

How unlike my encounter with that other great singer, Luciano Pavarotti (or rather with his entourage). This happened when the Italian was booked to do a one night stand at the Theatre Antique in Orange. (Incidentally, what a fascinating, as well as gigantic venue, that is. In addition to seeing Pavarotti and the Kirov Ballet, I've also seen the Chinese Circus, the Glenn Miller Orchestra and the Buena Vista Social Club there – and would have seen the marvellous Renée Fleming, but she cried off in favour of playing the Proms the following week.)

Tickets for the Pavarotti concert had sold like hot croissants but fortunately I had booked in good time. Anne and I were taking two friends from Brussels with us, Hywl and Movena Jones (Hywl was in charge of education and human resources in the EU Commission) and Georgette Penne, the mother of Guy Penne (the mayor of our village, Ste Cécile les Vignes). Reckoning that concerts in France never start on time, we had a leisurely dinner before proceeding to the theatre, thinking we had plenty of time. How wrong can you get? When we reached the theatre we had to climb loads of stairs and endure baggage checks before entering the arena and finding it was jam-packed, so tight that we could not get anywhere near our seats, which in any case were already occupied.

As we looked down at the vast arena we saw a mass of heads and shoulders looking like an unbroken carpet of enormous dimensions. Looked at from below, Peter Mayle, writing about the same concert (in *Toujours Provence*) said: "Thousands and thousands of faces, pale against the darkness, made row after row of semi-circles which disappeared up into the night." Whether looked at from above or below, the scene amounted to the same thing – a monument to lousy stewarding! Furious, especially because of the stress on our 93-year old guest, Hywl and I went in search of stewards who were as scarce as the audience was vast.

Eventually we found one steward who said she could do nothing and that we should speak to "that man over there", a uniformed official who also said he could do nothing and that we should speak to "that man in the white suit" two levels below. He turned out to be Pavarotti's PR man, but was equally useless. However, he did refer us to Tibor, Pavarotti's manager – he surely could not be impotent. But first he asked us what country we were from and when I told him we were British and, exaggerating somewhat, that my friend was in charge of education in Europe, he said, "Good, because we're not coming here again." We told him of our 93-year old friend and how it was tiring her, and how infuriating it was that we could not get anywhere near our 650 franc seats. He agreed and said he would fix things for us. First, he took us down to the wings and provided seats. The concert was about to begin with some whistling from equally aggrieved customers up in "the gods". At the interval, Tibor returned with five chairs and led us to a spot in front of the stage only yards from where Pavarotti would be singing. Some rows back, Guy Penne was sitting with Lionel Jospin, at that time the minister for education in the Mitterand government. He looked astonished as we and his mother walked in (he had paid 1,000 francs for his seats). We enjoyed the rest of the proceedings immensely, although the presence of heavies in front of the stage prevented me from filming the concert as I had hoped. But at least I got a recording of it on my camcorder.

I guess that's enough of the name-dropping (I suppose I could have mentioned the Queen and Prince Charles – but then, they're not musicians or artistes). But I must conclude by talking about a group of musicians who have given me as many thrills and as much pleasure as any of the greats I have referred to, and who have done that year after year for more than 20 years. The dates of their performances are the first entry in my new diary every year – the Schools Proms held at the Royal Albert Hall on three days each November, the culmination of a series of regional festivals around the country involving more than 30,000 youngsters aged from 5 to 21. Each night the Schools Proms feature symphony and chamber orchestras, brass and steel bands, trios, quartets and quintets, as well as swing and jazz bands, massed choirs and single choirs, dancers and a variety of soloists.

The quality and variety of their performances is, I believe, greater than that achieved by the children and young people of any other country in the world, an achievement of which Britain should be very proud. But how much does the country ever learn of them from our media? The answer is precious little, for the Schools Proms are generally ignored by the press, radio and television. This is, in my view, a national disgrace, especially where the BBC is concerned (though not Classic FM). The BBC regularly devotes hours of coverage to such festivals as Glastonbury and treats us to the spectacle of thousands of spectators waving and cheering frantically at the efforts of frequently far from top-rate musicians, but none of them are performing. They are simply spectators, whereas the thousands of youngsters who appear at the Schools Proms and its preceding festivals are displaying rich and varied talents which are a credit to their teachers and coaches, their parents, and above all to their own dedication. We hear enough from the media about the misdeeds of small, unrepresentative groups of youngsters, but virtually damn-all about our country's young musicians. One channel now tells us that "Britain's got talent" – it's about time that all sections of the media woke up and focused on the talents that have been developing for years among our youngsters across the country.

I'm not suggesting that people should not go to festivals which feature has-beens, third-raters and dubious foreign imports, as well as the highly talented, if that is what they want to do, or that some of that should not be featured in the media. But I do suggest that it would be less philistine and less shameful to the image of this country if greater prominence and encouragement were given to the talents and achievements of our young musicians – and of our young people in other fields as well.

Labour's very own paparazzo

"So you've reinvented yourself as a photographer,"
said Kenneth Baker as we chatted across the road
from Big Ben about one of my exhibitions some
time into my retirement. Ken had been my principal
adversary in the battles over teachers' pay in the
80s, having been brought in to replace Keith Joseph
who had been losing out to us on the PR front.
(Keith struck me as a very sensitive intellectual who
had no liking for the rougher side of politics. But he
was kind and courteous – and the only Tory to come
to my retirement party.) Ken was an altogether
tougher operator but he was not quite right about
my "reinvention" as a photographer. I had, in fact,
been involved with photography for years before
I finished at the NUT – it was just that in retirement
I could do so much more of it.

I had certainly had as much excitement and
enjoyment from my photography as I got from
many aspects of my day job. The great thing about
photography is that there are so many subjects or
objects to recapture, so many shapes and shades
of colour to reflect, that one has scarcely to step
outside one's own back door or one's own living
room to get outstanding pictures. And if one is
lucky enough to travel to other towns, cities or

countries, to witness or participate in exciting or historic events, to see or meet with figures on the world stage, one's opportunities for good photographs increase enormously. It is because, over the years, I have been fortunate enough to enjoy some of those opportunities, rather than because I am a particularly good photographer, that I have managed to take pictures which have interested other people to the point when I have been able to stage some ten exhibitions in a variety of places, show pictures at a number of events and place quite a few pictures in a number of publications and newspapers. For many years, and especially in my "retirement", I invariably took my camera with me. Whenever I did not have it, and particularly at union and political events, I've been greeted with "Where is your camera?"

I guess it was because of my snapping at Labour Party conferences, at Millbank and the Festival Hall in the 1997 general election, and at the general council's dinner at the Trade Union Congress, that on one occasion Tony Blair, then prime minister, referred to me as "Labour's very own paparazzo" (I was glad he didn't say "New Labour's").

My passion for photography did not get off to an early start. As a kid, apart from occasionally using the family box Brownie on holidays and on a school trip to Paris before the war, I did no photography at all. I was more into stamp collecting, reading books, and football. What aroused my interest was a stroke of luck when I was in military government in Germany after the war. The makers of Voigtlander cameras had resumed production and made some of their products available to the NAAFI, which in turn raffled some for the troops. I was fortunate enough to win one. Although film was hard to get at that time I did manage to get enough to take pictures of the war damage in Kiel and Hamburg, the first post-Hitler German elections – and my German girlfriends. But it was after I was demobbed and had become a student that my photography began in earnest, thanks particularly to the opportunities presented by my involvement in the National Union of Students in the early 1950s.

In those days it was difficult for non-Communists to travel freely in and around the Soviet Union and Eastern Europe, and not easy to take photos there wherever one wanted to.

I had some experience of those difficulties in 1950 when I went to Prague as an NUS delegate to the congress of the International Union of Students. On a free afternoon I went round old parts of the city and, coming across an attractive building, started to take pictures of it. After I'd taken some shots a hefty character in a leather overcoat came up and ordered me to go with him into the building. What was sinister about the situation was that as we went through the building the doors were locked behind us. After a long wait in one room a uniformed officer appeared and started to question me as to why I was in Prague and why I was taking pictures. I explained my presence at the congress (where our delegation came under great pressure because of NUS opposition to the Communists' perversion of the IUS) and that I thought the building was attractive and worth photographing. Fortunately I was not questioned about events at the congress but the film was removed from my camera – and not returned. Finally I was allowed to leave, thinking that the building probably was something more than a piece of attractive architecture!

I had another scaring experience on the way out of Czechoslovakia after the congress. The train passed through Brno and while it was stopped at the station I took pictures of some peasants on the platform tending their chickens. When we got to the frontier the train was stopped for some time and we wondered why. The reason became apparent as police walked along the train, looking in every compartment until they got to ours, when they saw my camera and told me to go with them to the frontier control. It would seem that someone had spoken to the authorities about my picture-taking. This time my explanation was accepted and the film was not removed. Greatly relieved, I was allowed to rejoin the train and we went on our way.

Four years later I led an NUS delegation on a visit to the Soviet Union. This time there was no problem about my photography – I guess it would have been difficult for our hosts to say that a delegation leader, however critical he might be, should not take shots of life in their country. Tom Blau's agency, Camera Press, bought a set of my pictures and the *Times Educational Supplement* published a page of them. With a bit of luck, my photographic career was launched.

While opportunities for photography can be limitless, inevitably certain topics or fields may appeal more than others. In my case the focus has been on political and trade union people and events, flowers and markets, foreign travel and, of course, family and friends. Much has been fostered by my life in the student and labour movements. However, when I started to use my own pictures for our Christmas cards and friends told me they collected them and displayed them, I thought maybe my photography wasn't too bad and might be of some wider interest. The first Christmas card picture I used was of a sunrise taken from a plane on my way from Australia, the next of the United Nations flag above the UN building in New York; but thereafter I always used flowers – from our own garden, the Chelsea and Hampton Court shows, Kew Gardens, the Paris Jardin des Plantes, Ste Cécile and Monet's garden. It was not until some years later that I thought of doing an exhibition, when events led me in that direction.

During the years of Tory rule between 1979 and 1997 the TUC and affiliated unions organised a number of marches and demonstrations on a variety of issues such as health service and education cuts, youth unemployment, local government legislation, and employment rights, as well as traditional events such as the Tolpuddle rally and the Burston School Strike march. On each occasion I took my camera and recorded the action. No event was more rewarding than the victory march to celebrate the lifting of the ban on trade union membership at GCHQ which the Tories had imposed in 1987. I had taken pictures of the first march through Cheltenham that year and the final march after the new Labour government had lifted the ban. That march took place in pouring rain and nothing signifies the spirit of union members more than the way they marched on through the town, drenched to the skin but determined to celebrate the occasion. It provided my best ever demo picture and I presented my picture of both marches to Brendan Barber and his wife on the occasion of Brendan's retirement as TUC general secretary.

My membership of the TUC general council provided a number of other photo opportunities. Particularly valuable was that offered by my roles as chairman of the TUC's nuclear energy review body. That led us to visit nuclear energy installations in Sweden and France as well as in Scotland. We also went to the Ukraine to discuss the Chernobyl disaster with the Soviet trade unions. I had wanted to take pictures of the reactor and the devastated site but Anne had not wanted me to go there so I stayed behind in Kiev for discussions with the Ukrainian ministers and officials. Other trips on behalf of the TUC were much less gruesome and took me to Kazakhstan, Leningrad, Moscow, Belgrade, Athens, Vienna, Berlin, Oslo and Melbourne; while on behalf of the NUT, I went to Singapore, Delhi, Bucharest, Volgograd, Helsinki, Stockholm, Copenhagen and Malta. On all the trips I took my camera with me.

Once I had retired I had more opportunities for photography but had no expectation at all of exhibiting my pictures. The suggestion that I ought to consider an exhibition arose as a result of what I did in connection with the 1997 general election.

In that election I was involved in dealing with education issues at Millbank, the Labour Party's election headquarters. In the course of that work I suggested to Tom Sawyer, the party's general secretary, that we were all engaged in what could prove to be an historic occasion and that it would be valuable to record what was going on in and around the campaign. Tom took the same view and agreed I could take pictures at Millbank and campaign events. I was allowed to capture all aspects of life at Millbank and was the only person to do so. In addition to my pictures at Millbank I accompanied John Prescott, the party's deputy leader, for a day on the campaign bus touring in the south-east. The high spot, of course, was the all-night celebration of Labour's victory at the Festival Hall and the most exciting moment came when I stood alongside John Prescott, Neil Kinnock, Peter Mandelson and others as they waited to greet Tony Blair on his arrival from his constituency. It was well worth losing a night's sleep to capture the joy of that momentous occasion.

Knowing I had taken a load of pictures of the general election and preceding events, a friend, Keith McDowell, suggested I should mount an exhibition of them. I said that if it were felt my pictures were good enough and that a site and a sponsor for an exhibition could be found I would be happy to organise it. Here, again, I was fortunate. I was introduced to David Evans (at the time the owner of Centurion Press) who was willing to sponsor the exhibition and the TUC was willing to provide the Marble Hall at Congress House as the site. (Successive general secretaries of the congress have allowed me to use the hall to launch all my exhibitions, support for which I am profoundly grateful.)

I decided that the content of the exhibition should not only cover the general election and preceding Labour Party events, and the marches and demonstrations of the Tory years, but also pictures from the Soviet Union and Eastern Europe, the fall of the Berlin Wall, and my first post-war pictures from Germany, student events and education. Before the end of 1997, "Days of Rallies and Roses" was ready and John Prescott, now deputy prime minister, opened it. In addition to the launch at Congress House it was later staged at Manchester town hall and Norwich city hall. Thus I began my venture into the mounting of photographic exhibitions and a widening of my photographic activities, that I had never contemplated when I started with my Voigtlander 50 years earlier.

I quickly followed "Days of Rallies and Roses" with a small exhibition at the Old Bull Theatre in Barnet. Entitled "Politicians, Poppies and Other Flowers", it contained some of my favourite flower pictures and that pointed me in another direction – to one of the world's most famous gardens, that of Claude Monet at Giverny. I paid two visits to the garden with its rich variety of blossoms, its incomparable clusters of water-lilies – and its ubiquitous hordes of Japanese tourists who left one waiting ages to get shots without them in the background. Thanks to sponsorship by Vivendi I was able to present my Monet exhibition in Birmingham City central library, Poole Arts Centre, Alton Gallery and the Institut Francais at Oxford, as well as London.

Preparing my next exhibition was a special treat – it involved covering all aspects of the life of West Ham United FC for a whole season in order to present "Homage to the Hammers". As a lifelong supporter of the club, what could be a more cherished assignment? I was delighted when Terry Brown, the then chairman of the club, agreed to the project and the Football Foundation agreed to join in financial support, the Professional Footballers Association agreed to pay for a reception to launch it, and the TUC provided a celebratory dinner. I could not have wanted more help than I was readily given and had access to every aspect of the club's many activities, including the board meeting. There was just one exception: the shot I most wanted but could not get was that of Harry Redknapp, the team manager, talking with his players in the dressing-room at half-time. "No-one else is ever allowed in there then, not even the chairman," said the PR man. So I had to settle for the referee and his assistants in their room instead. The exhibition was opened by one of West Ham's finest players, Sir Trevor Brooking. It was very well received and Newham Council had a special version of it made for exhibition in the borough's new public library and at a local festival.

My next exhibition involved another year devoted to a cherished institution – my old college at Oxford, St Catherine's. "Catz" was due to celebrate the 40th anniversary of its establishment as a college, following its previous existence as a society, and I suggested to the master, Peter Williams, that it might be appropriate to mark the occasion with an exhibition portraying life at the college. He agreed and in the course of the academic year I paid a number of visits to capture all aspects of life at Catz, academic and social. One very gratifying by-product of this project was that the college paid for me to go to New York to take pictures at the reception for American alumni organised by the university and its colleges. At the reception I got some excellent pictures of Bill Clinton (and a hand-shake from him as he passed down the line of guests). I was also able to get excellent pictures of the St Patrick's Day parade including a very moving tribute to the firefighters who died trying to rescue victims of 9/11. St Catherine's is now Oxford's largest college. It was a privilege to be allowed to illustrate its many qualities.

After I had done the exhibition my friend Tim Brighouse suggested I might do another one – on life in London schools. At the time Tim was acting as commissioner for London schools and directing the highly successful London Challenge. I was very happy to undertake such a venture and spent several months taking pictures in some 30 schools and colleges, one of which was on the site of the school I had attended as a kid more than 50 years earlier. It was an exciting assignment and every-where I received ready co-operation from staff and schools alike. The resultant exhibition was presented at the Royal Festival Hall and opened by Stephen Twigg, the minister for schools.

Another of my exhibitions which featured life in schools was derived from the National Teaching Awards. I went to all the schools in which the winners of the awards were teaching and took pictures of them at work with their pupils. The exhibition of those pictures was staged at the Department for Education: I hope its message was appreciated.

In another year I went to the magnificent Schools Proms presented by Music for Youth at the Royal Albert Hall. Over the three nights I took pictures of every group of performers, some 30 in all. It was an exhilarating experience and the pictures were displayed in the Festival Hall, sponsored by Marks and Spencer.

One could not spend more than 30 years holidaying in France without taking masses of photographs and, in my case at least, doing exhibitions too. I have written about them in Bonjour Ste Cécile, but some of them were also presented here in England as well.

My penultimate exhibition, "Photo Opportunities", was an attempt to convey a message to newcomers to photography – that there are so many things in everyday life which can yield good pictures just as well as big occasions. After its showing in London I was invited to take it to Gateshead civic centre, in the friendly north-eastern town at which I had put on the NUT's primary education touring exhibition decades previously. I was very fortunate that when "Photo Opportunities" was on show at Congress House, Mikhail Gorbachev was due to give an important speech in the Congress

Hall. Around that time the NUT had founded an appeal to help the Russian children who had been victims of the Chechen terrorist attack on their school, where many were killed or injured. I had offered to give some of my Russian pictures to raise money for the appeal and suggested it would help if Gorbachev would sign them when he came to Congress House. He readily agreed to do so and I was able to meet him and tell him about the origin of my pictures. It was great to meet a world figure whose influence on our lives has been so profound.

I had been intending to do another exhibition on the two Covent Gardens (the market and the opera house) and had secured the agreement of the authorities in both places to take pictures. Unfortunately my health problems put paid to that – at least for the time being.

I did, however, manage to organise my biggest and most productive exhibition, the purpose of which was to raise funds for the North London Hospice, the hospice which did so much for Anne before she died. It included all my best pictures and a number that had not previously been shown. The exhibition was opened by Sarah Brown, who made a very moving speech about the hospice movement, and Neil Kinnock auctioned the main pictures. The outcome was that it raised £7,300 for the hospice, to which I was able to add a further £500 – the fee I received for the use of one of my election pictures (of the late Philip Gould) in Tony Blair's book.

That was, for me, one of two very special occasions. The other was when I was invited to put on a small exhibition at the Photographers' Gallery in

London. Given the high standard of the exhibitions staged at the gallery, I was deeply grateful to have been given that opportunity.

While the bulk of my photographic activity has been wrapped up in the exhibitions, various other uses have arisen. Quite a few of my pictures have been used in publications, especially *Education,* the *TES, Education Guardian* and *The Times* and even, on one occasion, the *Daily Mirror.* And it was very pleasing to renew links with my old friend, Paul Cave, the great *Mirror* journalist, and to provide pictures for his excellent *Hampshire County Magazine.* Other pictures have been used in other people's exhibitions.

So it's been quite a journey since the far off days of the Voigtlander in post-war Germany. However, when I see the magnificent work of a world-renowned and truly great photographer – Sebastião Salgado – or the great pictures in the exhibition of landscape photography and the dramatic and often heart-rending pictures in the World's Press Now exhibition, I realise just how far I have to go before I get anywhere near the quality of such work. On the other hand, I have greatly valued and been excited by the chance to photograph some important moments and sites in history, such as the room from which Lenin ran the Russian revolution, the first post-Hitler elections in Germany and the first post-Communist elections in Hungary, the fall of the Berlin Wall with Russian troops standing by, the Holocaust memorial in the same city, and in this country the arrival of Tony Blair at the Festival Hall on the night of Labour's 1997 election victory, the march celebrating the lifting of the GCHQ ban, and the possibly unique picture of five leaders of the Labour Party together (and their signatures).

Then there has been the thrill of getting near enough to take pictures of one of the greatest figures of our time, Nelson Mandela, to meet and photograph Mikhail Gorbachev (another major figure who has profoundly affected our lives), and to get virtual studio-quality portraits of Bill Clinton (and shake hands with him twice!) and have him sign some of them to raise funds for the Labour Party; and altogether different subject, but one which produced a picture of near Cartier-Bresson quality, of postgraduate students in Leningrad in 1954; being able to capture the beauty and vivacity of Anne, the eagerness of children in schools and the inspiration of their teachers, the elegance of flowers and the dynamism of markets. Those are some of the reasons why one has a camera to hand, ready to seize the vital moments even if one is not Salgado, just "Labour's very own paparazzo".

Bonjour Ste Cécile

Tell anyone who knows something of France that you've "got a place in Provence" and the likelihood is that their eyes will light up and their interest is aroused. Doubtless they have memories (or visions) of clear blue skies and relentless sunshine, of lavender and mimosa, figs and olives, luscious peaches, abundant melons, huge tomatoes and *herbes,* coupled with recollection of the grandeur of the Pont du Gard and the Théâtre Antique in Orange, the Palais des Papes and that blessed *pont* in Avignon, the magnificent Arènes in Arles (and Van Gogh's old haunts), of great concerts in Aix and Choralies in Vaison-la-Romaine, of the nightmare of parking in Nice or Cannes or Saintes-Maries-de-la-Mer, and of *bouillabaisse* and crooks in Marseille.

Most of those delights still obtain but some things are not as they were – for example, you'll now hear plenty of talk about the extremes in the weather, of floods and storms and snowfalls not seen before, or at least not in living memory; and one finds the cuisine is no longer so superior to what is available in plenty of places in the UK. The *vignerons* still produce some excellent wine but are having a much tougher time selling it, prices are getting grim and unemployment grimmer, especially among the young. So that may lead to disappointment for some who have gotten a place in Provence, but that can depend on why they chose to get it in the first place.

Of course, we knew of and sought to enjoy the kind of delights I've mentioned; but there was also something else we sought and found and which I continue to enjoy (although sadly am unable to share with Anne) and that is the joy to be found in living in two different worlds and, to some extent, leading two different lives. I appreciate that one doesn't need to go to Provence to experience that joy: you could probably experience it in Timbuktu or Vladivostok or many other places too. But for us, for more than 30 years, it has been Provence and this is why, and what it has been like.

The idea of looking for a holiday home in France was Anne's entirely, and she had it long before it became a fashionable thing to do (spurred on by the cheap flights provided by Ryanair and Easyjet). Had it been down to me, I would have suggested she should use the money she inherited from the sale of her mother's flat to spend on holidays in different countries, but she loved France, it was her money, and I had already been to a number of countries with the NUS and the NUT. So it was a *maison secondaire* in France; then the question was – where?

We had already camped in various parts of France – in Normandy, Brittany, the Landes, the Dordogne, and on the Mediterranean coast at Sanary-sur-Mer, Cap d'Agde and Collioure, but we had also spent a holiday at the home of Guy Penne and his family at Sainte-Cécile-les-Vignes in northern Provence. Anne had got on very well with Guy's mother, Georgette, and that, plus the general charm of the village and the area, settled it.

Sainte-Cécile-les-Vignes "at the heart of the Côtes du Rhône" (it claims to be the biggest producer of its wine) was chosen and Guy, who was en route to becoming the mayor of the village, provided a list of houses that might be suitable. The one we liked most was the closest to the Pennes' house, which was a great help.

What we did not know until some time later, after discovering a red flag along with an assortment of helmets in the attic, was that its previous owner, Monsieur Roche (occupation *cantonnier* – a road mender) was an active Communist, which might have amused my old Stalinist opponents in the NUS as much as it did me. Equally amusing was that after we were installed in the house his daughter and her husband called to ask if we would pay for the coal they had left behind on leaving the house. Given that they had removed virtually all the furniture we were told we would find in the house, I told them we would not wish to pay the 400 francs they wanted for the coal, that we were not likely to need it and they were welcome to take it away in their car. They were miffed, and eventually I paid them 150 francs – and we are still using the coal today!

One of the consequences of living in two different worlds, and I guess it is almost inevitable, is that we have seen much more of our French friends in Provence than we have seen of most of our friends in England, though the other side of that coin is that, sadly, one sees more of one's friends in France passing on, or moving into the *maison de retraite,* providing a sobering pointer to the onward advance of ageing and the inevitable that comes with it, sooner rather than later. I'm blessed with the kindest of neighbours in both worlds who are unfailingly ready to help when their help is needed. What I like so much about coming to the same village year after year is the pleasure of walking down the street, passing through the market, entering shops and cafés, going to concerts and being greeted warmly and immediately feeling at home. There is also the joy of recognising and sharing a real sense of community, of vitality and forward-looking development. What a contrast to the tired and worn-out France of yesteryear, of the white, dusty, untarmacked roads of Provence tramped by Raimu in those pre-war Pagnol films, of the peeling wall posters advertising Dubonnet and the lousy phone system. What a contrast, also, to our borough of Barnet, with its "Easyjet council" closing libraries and cutting early years provision, creating a furore over parking charges and changing the secondary schools to "academies" because of their dissatisfaction with the council.

In the 30-odd years I've been coming to Ste Cécile I have seen what a dynamic and dedicated mayor and council can do for their fellow citizens and how real the sense of community is. Right-wing commentators in this country condemn what they call the "statism" of France, which they say kills personal responsibility and enterprise. I'm not going to generalise about the whole of France, but from my experience that kind of talk is nonsense so far as Ste Cécile is concerned, and that could well apply also to many other parts of the Republic, though maybe less so in the areas where the far right is in charge.

Over those 30 years Ste Cécile has established an excellent *collège*, which serves eight neighbouring villages, built an *école maternelle* and a *crèche*, and is now creating an education centre. It has also opened a splendid *boulodrome*, a big community centre, a library, a museum, an IT centre, a club for *ados* (teenagers), and built a fine *maison de retraite* (opened by President Mitterand) with the lowest charges in the area, while its market has grown into one of the best around.

Another achievement has been the creation of the new football stadium. This came about with the building of the new *collège*, which required the takeover of the village football pitch and its replacement with a new *stade*. When the council decided it should be called Stade Eric Cantona, who could be more appropriate to perform the opening than the great footballer himself? On the day of the opening Cantona arrived by helicopter from Marseille. As he came down to earth hundreds of eager kids rushed forward with their shirts and caps, anxious for him to sign them. I had promised the mayor that I would take photos of him with Cantona, which in due course I did. I told Cantona that I had seen him often on the telly when he played for Manchester United, and that I myself was a West Ham United fan. He immediately asked how the Hammers were getting on and was clearly aware of their problems at the time. I put him in the picture, and he offered his best wishes for the club. I then asked if he would sign my sun-hat, which he did – it now has pride of place in my wardrobe.

All those developments have been publicly provided or subsidised, but there is no lack of voluntary activity and enterprise in the village. Ste Cécile is a working village, not one that goes dead when the owners of *maisons secondaires* depart after their holidays. It has more than 50 voluntary organisations, clubs and societies catering for all kinds of interests – cultural, musical, artistic, sporting, religious, linguistic – and for all ages. All that, and *la chasse* too.

For a village of its size (really it is a small town), Ste Cécile is well endowed with shops and eating places, and its main road (the location for its market) is blessed with an avenue of *platanes* (plane trees) which provide welcome shade in the hot summer, making the heat bearable for the crowd that surges through the market. As bread matters so much to the French, it is good that there are three *boulangeries,* as well as two well-stocked grocers, a quality *boucherie,* a prosperous pharmacy (which pharmacy isn't?), an excellent bookshop and a fine garden centre, three estate agents, three banks and four *coiffeurs* – but as yet no nail shop.

The village is compact and all the shops and eating places are accessible, which means that one is not dependent on the hypermarkets of Bollene and Orange, which is a great help to us oldies (of which there are plenty among the inhabitants).

There is also a post office but, as I discovered when trying to trace an undelivered letter, it does not deal with the post these days.

In the centre of the village is Place Max Aubert, a spacious and attractive square that houses the *mairie*, the *office du tourisme*, the museum and the IT centre, and on market days is full of stalls to supplement those on the main streets. Across from the square are the well-kept but not too busy church, and the war memorial. It is an indication of the growth of Ste Cécile that it now has three good restaurants, an hotel, two pizzerias and three cafés, and a *crêperie* that serves meals at reasonable prices.

So good eating is to be had at a variety of places. But it is an even bigger treat to be invited to lunch or dinner with French friends. For not only is the food invariably excellent but one gets the additional enjoyment of listening to the guests and the cook discussing what went into the meal, how much of which ingredients, which herbs or oils and how long it all took. Fascinating stuff, and small wonder that food remains at the centre of the French way of life.

Given its claim to be the biggest producer of Côtes du Rhône wines, it is not surprising that the village has two large *caves coopératives* and several *domaines,* one of which is run by our friend Frederic, the son of Guy Penne. It is, however, a sign of the problems now facing many *vignerons* that some vines have been taken out of use and more are likely to follow.

Some of the developments I've described have been stimulated by population growth (it went up from 1,815 in 1980 to over 2,353) but since there is no major industry in the area other than the vineyards that dominate it, but that do not employ large numbers of people, it suggests that Ste Cécile's vitality and community spirit are an attraction in themselves. They are qualities which are certainly reflected in the pages of the excellent *Gazette* which the council distributes to every household six times a year. Very well designed and copiously illustrated, it records all aspects of life in the village, the activities of the mayor and council, and the achievements of its citizens. I wonder how many English towns or villages can point to such a service.

Equally, I wonder how many places in our country can point to the high level of participation in the events in its year's calendar. I've never lived in an English country town or village and it may be that such participation is what distinguishes rural from urban life, so I do not seek to contrast what happens in England with what I've seen in Ste Cécile over the years. But I do wonder how many places of comparable size in England would be likely to have 500 people sitting down to a banquet like Ste Cécile's to celebrate Bastille Day, and then have the same number come together again three days later for their saint's day? And how many of our rural communities do as they do in Ste Cécile and stage *Noël dans les Rues* at Christmas, when local shopkeepers provide food and drink for the citizens and Father Christmas, having abseiled down the clock tower, drives his sledge through the village and distributes sweets to the children?

I tried to capture some of the spirit and life of Ste Cécile in the first of three photographic exhibitions I staged at the town hall. It was entitled "20 years in the life of Ste Cécile as seen by an Englishman", and the mayor and council were kind enough to present me with a medal in recognition of it. The other exhibitions portrayed market day and the *Ban de Vendanges* (the start of the grape harvest), and Monet's garden.

I must say they are pretty generous with the presentation of the village medal. Anne and I received one when we celebrated our 40th wedding anniversary in Ste Cécile, and another when we celebrated our golden wedding there. But more importantly, seven of the council's staff were presented with medals at the last Bastille Day banquet in recognition of their long service to the community. Gestures like that contribute to the community spirit of the village. What reinforces it is the number of events that bring the inhabitants together in addition to the annual festivities. Events like the mayor's town meeting at which he reports on the year's activities, the *vide greniers* when folks bring their bric-a-brac to sell, the *Fête du Rosé* which attracts some 2,000 people, the cinema shows (including outdoor ones in the summer) and concerts like those that form part of the series of *Musique dans les Vignes* which was launched by Guy Penne 20 years ago.

Although I've talked about living two lives in two different worlds, it could be that our presence in Ste Cécile over the decades has made a contribution, albeit a small one, to promoting good relations between our two countries. At least that is what the local press has said on a number of occasions when it has reported on parties we have held for our French friends and visiting friends from England. *"Au rendez-vous de l'amitié France-Angleterre"* said one headline, while another spoke of *"La double nationalité de Fred Jarvis"* (but don't tell UKIP). The papers also reported how Anne and I had presented ourselves before the mayor for a *mariage républicain* on the occasion of our golden wedding anniversary and our having been made *Cityoens d'Honneur de la Commune.* It has certainly been an enormous pleasure to entertain many friends from England and to find they have liked the village as much as we have.

Two of those friends have been the writer Julian More and his wife Sheila. We met them not long after finding the house in Ste Cécile. They were living in a lovely house in the nearby village of Visan and Julian had written *View from a French Farmhouse,* a fine book about the area which was beautifully illustrated with the superb photographs of his daughter, Carey. That was followed by a number of other excellent books about life in France, including one on French cuisine which won an award in France. We had some very enjoyable times with them in Visan and Ste Cécile. Sadly, Julian died three years ago, and when I spoke at his funeral in Marseille I said how superbly and sensitively he had conveyed the spirit of France in his books, in contrast to the books of Peter Mayle. I was not aware that Mayle was also present, but I would still have said that if I had known. It would have been great if Julian had written about Ste Cécile for he would have done it more fittingly than me. But I hope I have conveyed something of the life and character of the village and have shown why, when I talk about Provence, I don't dwell on those delights and features which I certainly appreciate, but on the values and spirit of community which we have found in our "other world". It may be we're lucky in that Ste Cécile is, and has been, led by a progressive council and a succession of very able and far-sighted mayors. The same may not apply in some other parts of Provence, but I am sure Julian would have agreed about our good fortune, nevertheless.

Homage to the Hammers

"The loyalty of players is what it is. The loyalty that really matters to any football club is the loyalty of the fans. Fred, you're a good example of that loyalty. From a lad over the years you've seen thousands of players come and go and you've remained steadfast in your loyalty. It's in the genes," said David Gold, the co-owner and co-chairman of West Ham United FC, as we talked in the players' lounge at the Boleyn Ground.

To emphasise his view of loyalty, David told me of a conversation he had had with a six year old boy. After they had talked about the club he asked the boy how long he had been a supporter of West Ham. "All my life," declared the lad proudly.

Our family has links with and loyalty to the Hammers that have existed somewhat longer than those six years. In fact they go back nearly 90 years to the time when my father was one of the crowd of 200,000 souls who sought to see the FA cup final between West Ham and Bolton Wanderers which was the first to be played in the new Wembley Stadium (in 1924). Dad hadn't gone to see the renowned copper on that white horse who tried valiantly to control the crowd, but he didn't even get that far, so vast was the crowd. However, he recovered sufficiently from his disappointment to take me, ten years later, to see my first West Ham game at the Boleyn Ground.

Thus began the trips by tram from Custom House to Upton Park with Dad on those Saturdays when his shift work allowed and he was not too tired. Armed with a bag of peanuts (remember them?) bought from a bloke with a basket, and a packet of paregoric tablets to sustain us through the match (no jumbo hot-dogs or hamburgers in those days), we would make our way with difficulty through the crowd to the furthest corner of the ground. We were never in time to see the kick-off. Happily, because of the slope of the North Bank I was usually able to see most of the game, aided sometimes with a box to stand on.

When I am asked by those who don't know my background, "Why do you support West Ham?" I reply "Because I was born there" – as if there could be any other answer. As one former manager of West Ham, Ted Fenton, put it: "West Ham was our club, East London's club. I'm a cockney, not a proper cockney, but still a cockney, and that is what West Ham is."

Of course it is not obligatory for a Hammers supporter to be a cockney (my wife Anne was a fervent supporter, and she came from Oxford), but just as most cockneys wouldn't dream of supporting any other team (who said "Leyton Orient"?), so as Charles Korr (author of *West Ham United*) said: "It is impossible to imagine the Hammers outside East London. Clubs like West Ham not only create traditions and a sense of permanency, they are also their captives. A strong sense of shared loyalty exists between the supporters, local residents and the club."

Part of the madding crowd

The Tottenham Hotspur player Danny Blanchflower once said: "West Ham gets 26,000 cockneys turning up every week and they sing Bubbles on good days and bad, and they don't believe any other club exists." He was right, of course, but would it not be true of every other club's supporters too? When I met David Gold I asked him how the Hammers' supporters compared with those of Birmingham City, the club that he and David Sullivan owned before they took over at West Ham. He said, "Birmingham's supporters are passionate, but West Ham's are very passionate."

Very passionate indeed, and somewhat partisan too. But that is hardly surprising: we're not a bunch of academics at a seminar, seeking (but not necessarily succeeding) to be dispassionate and objective. Before every game, and again at half-time, we're urged to "get behind the lads", and get behind them we do, especially when they're flagging or losing. There are times when some of the Hammers' supporters go beyond the partisan, but not often in recent years, and then it's usually to question the ref's judgment – or parentage. Some years ago one of my best mates gave up his season ticket because he was sickened by what he considered the foul and sometimes racist remarks of some of those around him. His seat was not far from ours, but even then I didn't hear that kind of language where we were. Nowadays there is little of that kind of language and one reason for that could be the very significant increase in the number of women and children in the stands.

Sadly we get fewer of the cockney wisecrackers we used to hear, and while there is still the occasional stupid booing of a former West Ham player who has joined another club, there are also times when a former player gets warm applause when he no longer wears a claret and blue shirt.

I find it especially heartwarming to see so many young boys (and girls) coming with their dads (and mums too) to the matches, and a big factor in that will be the "Kids for a quid" scheme which West Ham has pioneered, and which is now widely regarded as a success. Clearly such a scheme costs the club money, but it is surely a wise investment for the future.

Moore than a football club

To the millions for whom West Ham United is not much more than a line on the football results at five o'clock on a Saturday afternoon, and perhaps a five minute spell on Match of the Day the same evening, the Hammers' slogan "Moore than a Football Club" may mean very little. And even to many of those who spend their Saturday afternoons watching the team it may not mean much more. It is only when one has fully read the club's excellent match-day programme, or had the opportunity to see at first hand the aspects of the club's life and services, that one can appreciate how justified that slogan is.

As David Gold said to me, West Ham is a community club and I first appreciated that when I spent a season photographing all aspects of the club's life for my exhibition "Homage to the Hammers". But that was 12 years ago and since then the club's activities have been extended, and are likely to be developed further when it moves to the Olympic stadium. Of course most football clubs have links with their local community, but I doubt whether any is more deeply embedded in its community than West Ham United. The club was, after all, born out of a local enterprise, starting life as Thames Ironworks FC, with its players coming from among the firm's employees. Since then, with the passing of 118 years, there have been many changes in the host borough. West Ham has become Newham; its population grew to 250,000 but was halved by the bombing which shattered the homes and workplaces of many of its inhabitants. In the post-war period the composition of its population has changed radically to the point where today it has a majority of non-white inhabitants. But none of these changes has altered the club's commitment to make an even bigger contribution to the life of the community. The fact that the club's new owners have such strong links with West Ham will surely mean that is even more likely to happen.

A look at the club's services shows how important it has become to Newham and East London generally. For example, with 400 employees it is now one of the biggest employers in the area.

Its hotel and corporate facilities and extensive marketing of a wide range of merchandise online and through its shops, generates trade as well as income, and reaches far beyond the Boleyn Ground.

For many years the club has catered for hundreds of youngsters through the organisation of a variety of coaching courses and, in addition, it provides an education centre which works with local schools. It has been involved in a number of projects such as the Gateway Project and does much charitable work, most notably in respect of the Richard House Children's Hospice. All this work will be enhanced with the move to the Olympic stadium. Karren Brady, the vice-chairman, has said that the Community Development Trust will ensure that the Queen Elizabeth Olympic Park will be a hub for education and sport for the community.

There is likely to be a significant increase in the size of the crowds watching the Hammers' games and also a change in their age composition. Already the club has reported a 23% increase in the number of young people coming to Premier League matches at Upton Park, and that is before the access schemes to which the club is committed. They will offer 100,000 free and affordable tickets to the most deprived community groups.

Already the club's Kidz Club project, a campaign which uses football to bring deprived communities together, has engaged 18,000 youngsters from Newham and Tower Hamlets, with even greater numbers expected next season. Karren Brady expects that the appointment of an experienced new head of community will bring a big expansion in the community department and its activities.

While the club is set in a multi-ethnic community, so far that has not been reflected in the complexion of the crowded terraces. In particular one does not see many Asian faces, although outside the ground and nearby are shops selling a dazzling array of saris and other Asian garments, markets selling a variety of exotic fruit and vegetables, and a cinema that shows only Asian films. It may be that Asians prefer cricket to football, but the club itself makes a determined effort to involve all sections of the community. The Asians in Football project aims to encourage young Asians of all abilities (girls as well as boys) to participate in football through coaching sessions. It has arranged matches with Bangladeshi teams and recently hosted the finals of the UK Asian Community Cup.

I am sure that all these developments will show how right David Gold is to say that West Ham United is a "community club" and how justified is the slogan "Moore than a football club".

The ups and the downs

At the party when Anne and I celebrated our golden wedding I said, "Over the years we have experienced many ups and downs – but then, that's what you come to expect as a loyal supporter of the Hammers."

There were times, first in the days when West Ham struggled to escape from the old Second Division, and more recently when we gained promotion to the Premier League and suffered relegation from it, when loyalties were stretched; but today the club stands on the verge of the biggest "up" in its 118 year history – the impending move to the Olympic stadium.

When I met David Gold there could be no mistaking his enthusiasm for the move and the eagerness with which he is looking forward to it, feelings which are clearly shared with his co-owner, David Sullivan, and their dynamic vice-chairman, Karren Brady, who is overseeing the preparations for the move with imagination, sensitivity, and great ability.

For those, like me, whose spectating began on the cold windswept and roofless North Bank in pre-war days, the transfer to one of the world's best known and most attractive sporting venues will seem a bit like contemplating a trip to the moon, even though the club's new home is only a mile from the spot where it began its existence as the Thames Ironworks FC all those years ago.

I had my misgivings about the move to the stadium; not for any doubt about the excellence of the site and the building, but because I felt it would be too big and would lack the atmosphere we get at the Boleyn Ground; and because, on personal terms, I felt that if I should still be around by the time of the move I would not get as good a view of the game as I get from my present seat. But David Gold sought to be reassuring on that point and indicated there would be steps to provide equivalent places for existing ticket holders. He was also reassuring when I asked about those present-day features that give character and colour to Upton Park – all the stalls with their scarves and hats, badges and old programmes, as well as the purveyors of hot dogs, meat pies, hamburgers and chicken legs, humbugs and all sorts (but no peanuts). Gold said there would be facilities at the stadium and it would be for traders to make use of them, though he recognises that in such big changes there were invariably winners and losers.

In any case, the move to the stadium, as I've already indicated, offers big opportunities in many directions, as well as the prospect of the increased income which the co-chairmen confidently expect. It could elevate West Ham United into a league of its own as the club that will sustain the aura of one of the most successful sporting events ever held in this country. Let us hope that the quality of football our players provide will be equal to our expectation.

If the biggest "up" in the history of West Ham United FC is the impending move to the Olympic stadium, usually the "downs" we have known are those that are experienced by most clubs at some time or other and generally they relate to the team's loss of form, the departure or prolonged injury of key players, or a spell in the danger zone when relegation threatens or, worse still, actually happens. While we Hammers supporters have known quite a few of these things over my 80 years as a fan, there has been one "down" which could have had much more severe repercussions for the club – it occurred four years ago and related to its financial position.

In this respect, also, West Ham's supporters have not been the only ones to have cause for concern. For such is the nature of the financing of professional football nowadays that there can be serious difficulties even for the most successful clubs (in footballing terms) and not just those in leagues below the Premier League. As David Sullivan has said, "Football is getting deeper and deeper in debt every year. Most Premier League clubs are deeply in debt and getting worse."

West Ham United has never been a wealthy club and is not known for lavish spending, but the first signs of financial difficulty came when the planned expansion of the ground's seating capacity was abandoned following the completion of the Doc Marten stand. That was followed by the change of ownership assumed by Icelandic interests. But far from improving, the financial situation deteriorated further and to such an extent that the club faced the prospect of passing into administration and having to sell its best players. Had that happened, the descent into a spiral of decline which has happened to some other clubs might have hit the Hammers. One wondered whether some oligarch or oil rich potentate or super speculator might come to the rescue, but there was no sign of one.

There must have been plenty of Hammers supporters who shared my relief when it was reported that David Sullivan and David Gold were going to buy the club. And I imagine I was not the only fan who wondered who they were and how they had become wealthy enough, first to buy Birmingham City FC and then to buy our club.

They were said to be "life-long supporters of the Hammers" and there was also talk of them being "porn kings".

In his book, *Pure Gold,* David Gold has spoken of his early venture into the publishing of "erotica" and his later acquisition, together with his brother Ralph, of the chain of Ann Summers stores of which there are 145 today with an annual turnover of £150 million. And David Sullivan has spoken of how he and Gold were denied a seat on the board of West Ham United FC more than 20 years ago, when they had 27% of the club's shares, because of the dislike the old guard (Hills and Cearns) had for their links with the sex industry. But nothing should be allowed to detract from the fact that it was the two Davids who saved the club four years ago. They do not talk in those terms themselves but that is what they did and that is why we, the supporters, should be profoundly grateful to them.

Furthermore, unlike the magnates who own other football clubs in this country, they can truly claim to have had a life-long attachment to West Ham and, uniquely in David Gold's case, to be almost certainly the only proprietor or chairman of an English club who was once offered the chance to play for his club. It is worth saying how this happened.

David Gold was born and brought up in Green Street, within a stone's throw of the Boleyn Ground. As he puts it, "from my place in poverty across the road in Green Street, I could always see the West Ham stadium – it was my portal to the wonderful world of football." Together with his brother and

263

mother, he lived in real poverty and with virtually no help from his father, who David has said was "a spiv and a petty criminal". David was dyslexic and his schooling was affected by ill-health but he shone at football. He was not only a leading player for West Ham Boys (in my time one of the best schoolboy teams in the country) but was also selected for South England Boys. Such was his ability that the manager of West Ham United invited him to sign forms for the club. He was bitterly disappointed when his father refused to sign the forms and thereby shattered his boyhood dream of playing for the Hammers.

When we met, David asked me what school I attended in West Ham. When I said Plaistow Sec in Prince Regent's Lane he said, "That was the posh school for bright kids. I went to Burke Secondary Modern, the school for the dummies." "Well you've not done so badly then," I said. In view of his successes in business and the fact that he gained a pilot's licence, and flies his own plane and helicopter, I saw David as a classic example of the folly of the 11-plus exam. So I asked him what he thought of selection at 11. He said it was not right, and it was unfair.

I have no doubt that David Gold's background and his links with the club that he and David Sullivan now own make him unique among football club proprietors, and that David Sullivan's commitment to the club is as strong and his acumen and experience as important to it.

Those of us who had real anxieties about the Hammers' future just a few years ago can take reassurance from the improvements that the new co-owners have already effected, their assertion that the business is now on a firm footing, and their confidence that the club's external debts will have been cleared before the move to the Olympic stadium. They also anticipate a substantial increase in the club's income when the stadium becomes the club's home, and that is even more reassuring.

Play up and play the game

While the two Davids have already done a great deal for the club they must surely recognise, as we supporters should too, that a good deal will also depend on the quality of the players and their ability to produce football worthy of the magnificence of their future surroundings. So how will they match up to the achievements of our past and present heroes? To be frank, in the pre-war and early post-war years there were not many players of top quality in the Hammers teams. My memory isn't what it was, but the only players I can recall being impressed by were Len Goulden, Jimmy Ruffell, Jim Barrett, Stan Morton and Ernie Gregory. In those days there were no black or brown faces, no foreign accents, and even the arrival of a Scot was something of an event, but then Archie Macaulay was also a very good player. Unlike today, the players seemed to stay much longer (and sometimes too long) at Upton Park. There also seemed to be fewer injuries, or we heard less about them, although whether that was because the play was less robust or the players more tough, I'm not sure. But I do remember that when a player got injured in those days it was Charlie Paynter, the manager, who rushed on in his raincoat and trilby carrying what looked like a doctor's bag, to administer the smelling salts. There were no paramedics in those days and while there was the large, communal hot bath after the match I don't think there was anything like the team of physios and sports psychologists and the impressive array of equipment I saw, that is on hand to take care of players today.

Certainly the general quality of the Hammers' squad has, in my view, become appreciably better than it was in those days, and in the last 20 years markedly so, though there have been some variations.

What everybody connected with the Hammers is entitled to be proud of is the number of outstanding players who have come up through the club or who have been brought in to play for it. Pride, too, that the Hammers have been to five FA cup finals. My Dad didn't get into Wembley in 1924, but Anne and I saw the Hammers win there on three occasions – against Preston North End, Fulham and Arsenal – and win the European Cup Winners Cup in one of the finest games I have ever seen. In their fifth FA cup final they were narrowly beaten by Liverpool, in what was one of the finest games in years.

Perhaps the greatest pride, however, should be felt in the fact that the only England team to win the World Cup was captained by Bobby Moore, arguably our finest player and England's best captain, and that he was partnered by the winning goal scorer, Geoff Hurst, and Martin Peters, also

Hammers players at the time. Later they were followed by such top quality players as Trevor Brooking, Julian Dicks, Billy Bonds, Tony Cottee, and Alan Devonshire. More recently still there have been outstanding players who began their careers at West Ham before going on to play for big clubs and for England, such as Rio Ferdinand, Frank Lampard, Michael Carrick, Paul Ince, Glen Johnson and Joe Cole (who has now returned to Upton Park). When David Gold spoke of the thousands of players seen in my 80 years as a supporter, all those players were among those who it was thrilling to watch. There have also been a number of outstanding players who have come to Upton Park in their twilight years but who were still capable of playing brilliantly, players like Stuart Pearce, Nigel Winterburn and Teddy Sheringham; while among some fine overseas players, who could ever forget the magnificent and untiring efforts of Carlos Tevez?

In the course of those 80 years there have been quite a number of players who came from West Ham or East London or nearby parts of Essex, and the club's academy has done a splendid job in developing promising youngsters. It was good to hear from David Gold that the academy will continue to play its part in such development, although he and David Sullivan are right to point to the fierce competition between clubs there is nowadays in the search for young talent and more agents "giving parents things" to attract them.

While the increased income the co-owners expect to come from the move to the Olympic stadium should make it possible to recruit new players of the calibre of our past heroes, nobody should have any illusions as to the ferocity of the competition to be faced. Nor should we forget the sad consequences that can arise when the club secures a top quality player only for him to suffer an injury that ends his career all too soon. The Hammers have known that too.

At the races

The many bookmakers who have benefited over the years from my investments with them have my dear friend, the late Jack Ashley, to thank for their good fortune. For it was the great campaigner and parliamentarian who introduced me to horse racing and the intricacies of betting.

Jack and I had first met when we were members of the national executive of the Labour Party's student organisation, NALSO. We lost touch for a time but met again when Jack had become a BBC producer and was working on a series about class in Britain. He wanted to film a typical working/middle class family and asked if we would help. We agreed, and in the course of his visits to our home in Finchley (where he later became the Labour candidate for Parliament) we talked about our camping holidays and an excellent site we had found near Salcombe in Devon. Jack said that he and his family were keen to go camping, so we invited them to join us the next time we went to Devon. When we were there Jack discovered that there was horse racing at Newton Abbot. He was keen to go, and asked if we would like to join him and his family. Until that time I had never been to a race meeting, nor bet on any horse. Anyway, we were game for the trip so we had a great, but (betting-wise) not very fruitful, day at Newton Abbot.

It's hardly the Ascot of the south-west, or even as good as Alexandra Park used to be (and that's saying very little), but the weather was fine and the company jolly. To really participate, however, it was necessary to know how to bet and how to get a fair deal from the bookies (as if that's ever possible). So Jack gave us an introductory course and, in particular, told me about the "yankee" – a device whereby one chooses horses in four or five races and combines them in doubles, trebles and accumulators, and where from a relatively modest outlay one can sometimes win a reasonable sum – if all four or five horses win or get placed. Given those possibilities, which sometimes occur, that has been the main betting device I've used ever since.

I daren't try to calculate how many times over all the years the "yankee" has not delivered (as they say, it's the bookie who has the Rolls Royce, not the punter), but it is good fun and can lead you into detailed study of the form of horses – and jockeys if you want to be serious. I have never betted without studying such form even though I know there are those, women in particular, who are inclined to bet on the basis of a horse's name or a jockey's racing colours.

So it all started with Jack at Newton Abbot. After the holiday there were times when Jack and I would go to Sandown Park or Kempton or Epsom, and we would frequently compare notes on our respective successes, or more often failures, with the nags. We would also compare notes with another friend (and another fine campaigner), Alf Morris, who was also very knowledgeable about the racing scene.

I won't say that since those days I've never looked back. Financially I would have been better off if I'd never gone to Newton Abbot, but on the other hand I've had enormous enjoyment on many occasions when I've watched great horses and determined jockeys involved in exciting contests on the turf. For I find racehorses are magnificent creatures and absolutely thrilling when they approach the winning post, all out to win. Some years ago I was going to make them the subject of my next photographic exhibition and Jenny Pitman, then a trainer, said she would let me visit her stables. Unfortunately, I developed a hernia problem and had to abandon the project.

Since that visit to Newton Abbot, I've been to a good many race meetings and, happily, Anne quite liked going too, as did Robin and Jacky. My favourite courses are Ascot and Sandown Park, and in recent years I've been more often to Hereford and Towcester which, like Newton Abbot, have a delightful countryside atmosphere.

While I was with the union there were times when I was able to link a visit to a racecourse with a speaking engagement, especially in the north-east where Bob Dargavel, the union's regional officer for the region and one of the finest officials I ever worked with, was a regular visitor to Gosforth Park. There also times, when I was attending a conference or union celebration abroad, when I would try to get to a race-meeting. That way I got to the Curragh and Bellestown in the Irish

Republic – I've never seen so many priests as I saw there (other than at the Cheltenham Festival) – and in France I got to Auteuil, Longchamp and Chantilly.

The visit to Chantilly was a riot – literally. I suppose the course is the Parisians' Ascot, though not on quite the same scale. On leaving the train from Paris it was necessary to take a path leading on to the course. As I followed the race-goers along the path I saw in the distance a crowd waving placards and flags, walking from the other end and approaching the stands. They were shouting slogans and waving their banners, which I thought was odd because the racing hadn't even begun. It soon became clear that they were determined to prevent the racing from starting: they were stable employees who were demonstrating against the trainers and owners over their pay. There are times when on some of our racecourses the crowd might get worked up, but I've never seen them do what these guys started to do. First they tried to pull down the railings surrounding the seating enclosures and then the authorities decided to let the races begin, doubtless expecting that would cause the demonstrators to disperse; but they didn't. Instead, when the runners for the first race sped down the course the demonstrators tried to pull the jockeys off their horses (and I don't think it was in anger over a losing bet). They meant business. The authorities decided to abandon the meeting, and I returned to Paris almost certainly better off financially than if the races had been run.

My other visit to a French course, apart from local meetings in Provence when on holiday, was when Anne and I were given a retirement present from the board of Stoke Rochford Hall in the shape of a weekend in Paris for the Arc de Triomphe, the biggest race in the French calendar. From our place in the stand we were able to see President Mitterand and his entourage, well away from the crowd. By contrast, when I went to Sandown Park to see the mighty Desert Orchid run, I was able to stand alongside the Queen Mother and her trainer, studying the horses. It didn't bring me luck with the bookies but I did get some good pictures of the Queen Mother – and Desert Orchid.

There was also the occasion when Brighton race-course staged a meeting linked with the Labour Party conference. All Labour's "royalty" turned up for the occasion – the Blairs, the Prescotts, etc. Whether they had a clue how to pick winners I don't know, but I got some good pictures of them too.

Part 4: 'Fred's Red'

It was not politics that brought Anne and me together. If anything, they might have kept us apart. Before I got to Oxford, Anne was already there at St Anne's College, studying PPE, and had soon become involved in the university's Socialist Club. She became, in turn, social secretary, treasurer, secretary, and finally, chair. But the Socialist Club was affiliated to the Student Labour Federation, a fellow-traveller body proscribed by the Labour Party. I, on the other hand, had started the Labour Society at Liverpool in opposition to the Socialist Society which was also affiliated to the SLF. There was, therefore, not much chance that I would be going to the Socialist Club meetings in which Anne was involved. Nor was I likely to be invited to the tea parties she organised, which *Isis* said were "bigger, and warmer and friendlier, and lasted longer than anyone else's".

And I would have been even less likely to get involved in the gatherings her parents held in various Oxford pubs. In that respect, and quite a few others, Anne's upbringing and family background was markedly different from mine. Her father, Reggie, was a member of a well-known Oxford family, the Colegroves, and he managed part of the family business, Hall the Printer, and that brought him into contact with a lot of undergraduates because the firm printed most of the posters for the university's many clubs and societies (as well as the programmes of Headington FC). Reggie had been at Jesus College while Anne's mother, Maureen, hailed from Norwich and in later life worked for the brother of Lloyd George and then

had a key post at Oxfam in Oxford. She had decidedly left-wing views and was a good deal less tolerant of other people's views than Anne was. In
addition to their undergraduate friends, another
of their drinking companions was the greatly celebrated, and much given to celebrating, poet Dylan
Thomas. When Maureen died we found, among her
papers, a song Dylan had given to her and which
had not previously been published. It was written
in Hesky's Long Bar in High Holborn in 1951 – how
apt it seems:

When Mr Watts-Ewers
(Licensed to sell
Beer, wine and spirits
And tobacco as well)
Admitted in the public
He would open that night
His brand new Hotel
The town had a fright

Mr Alf Measure
Who kept the Bull's Head
Wept like a baby
And took to his bed

Mrs Lil Jenkins
Of the old Pig and Swill
Sacked all the barmaids
And was sick in the till

In every saloon
And public too
There was such a commotion
As nobody knew

For Mr Watts-Ewers
(Licensed for all
Drinking and Smoking
By man small and tall)
Had decided to call
His Hotel the Liberty
Flibberty Gibberty
Libberty Hall – Hotel!

Oh! All Drinks were free
(And Cigarettes as well)
In Mr Watts-Ewers'
Brand new Hotel

There were no set hours
There were no decrees
And nobody started
Time Gentlemen Please

For Mr Watts-Ewers'
Splendiferous place
No Gentleman ever
Staggered our fair race

There was nothing to pay
And nothing to lose
In Mr Watts-Ewers'
Buckingham Palace of Booze.

The song has now been authenticated as the work of Dylan Thomas by Professor John Goodby of Swansea University who has included it in his new edition of the *Complete Poems of Dylan Thomas.* Professor Goodby notes that the song reflects Dylan's habit of occasionally composing impromptu pieces in pubs and clubs. "Slight though it is," says Professor Goodby, "it... is an amusing reflection on British pub culture of the time. Watts-Ewers's establishment is unlikely to have existed; his name is almost certainly a play on the traditional question posed when offering to buy someone a drink (What's yours?)."

Anne's parents were both interested in politics and Maureen was at one time a Labour candidate for the local council. There can be little doubt that Anne's early involvement in political activities after she had left her convent school for Oxford will have been much influenced by her parents, and especially by Maureen.

Fortunately for me, Anne's interests and activities were not confined to the Socialist Club. She sang in the Bach Choir, was on the committee of OUIDA, the Oxford University Intercollegiate Debating Society, and, most importantly, the Oxford NUS committee of which she became chairman (and of which, incidentally, Peter Brooke, a future Tory home secretary, was a member). I was already a member of the NUS national executive, having been elected to it while I was at Liverpool, and so I joined the committee. In spite of the major division over IUS which existed in the NUS at national level, we had few disagreements in the Oxford committee and

I developed a close friendship with Anne. The fact that we held different attitudes to the SLF did not impede it.

After graduating in 1951, Anne was awarded a fellowship in rural sociology at Reading University, but she was able to continue her involvement in the NUS.

I continued at Oxford for another year, having been awarded a research studentship at Barnett House (the delegacy for social studies) and had moved up in the NUS executive to become deputy president. I then prepared to run for the presidency and sought a team for the executive which I hoped would be more representative of the membership than the existing one. Because of Anne's links with the SLF I did not feel able to include her on my ticket, but she was popular enough to win a place and become a member of my first executive, and fully supported me in its work. We were, and I think remain, the only couple to have served together on the NUS executive – we became engaged, and married in August 1954, while I was still president.

Our wedding took place in the Oxfordshire village of Stanton Harcourt, where Anne lived with her parents in a delightful 17th century thatched cottage across the road from a working farm. With its large garden, it was later to prove a fun place for our children with much more scope than the back yard of my parents' terraced house in Wallasey – though we were able to take them to swim in the Mersey at the "beach" at Egremont as the big ships went by (they had some in those days).

We not only had the NUS to thank for bringing us together but also, indirectly, for finding our first home. Before we married Anne was living in Exeter doing her rural sociology research for Reading and I was living in the NUS flat. We had had no time to look for somewhere to live and I was due to go to the Soviet Union, leading an NUS delegation. One of the great characters at the NUS office was the charlady, "Mrs M" (a dead ringer for ITMA's Mrs Mopp). Before I left for Moscow, "Mrs M" asked me if we had found anywhere to live, and when I told her we hadn't even begun to look she said she would see what she could get from "next door", where she also "did" for the solicitors Scadding and Bodkin (I didn't make that up). To my astonishment, when I returned from Moscow three weeks later, she had indeed found us a place, a flat in Finchley. I wouldn't have made Mrs Thatcher's constituency my first choice, but with only three weeks to the wedding we could only be grateful and thank "Mrs M" for her great help.

After Jacky and Robin were born we moved to Barnet, and lived in the same house for the rest of our married life. It was in Barnet that Anne spent the whole of her 30-year teaching career, carried out all her work for the NUT and the Labour Party, and served for eight years as a councillor and chair of the borough's education and children's committees.

When our children were both old enough to go to school, Anne decided she would like to take up teaching, saying she had been inspired to do so by *I Want to Go to School*, the documentary film the union had made. But although she was a graduate she would first have to have some training. She and her friend Rosalyn Green, another Oxford graduate, wrote a letter to the *Guardian* urging the need for a course for graduates like themselves, and in response to that letter, Het Brookes, a former HMI, said she would be willing to organise such a course if a college could be found to provide the necessary facilities. Eric Robinson, principal of Enfield College of Technology, was prepared to provide those facilities, and before long the course was launched and proved of great benefit to a substantial number of graduates. It was after that course that Anne began her teaching career at Northside School in Finchley. Rosalyn Green also taught at the school, before going on to become a very successful head teacher. Anne stayed at Northside until her retirement, but in addition became a leading member of the Barnet Teachers' Association. She was elected president of the association and then membership secretary. She was a regular and forthright delegate at the union's annual conferences, and did not hesitate to criticise the national executive when she felt that necessary.

There was one occasion when she delighted the women delegates, but perhaps not all the men, by rebuking the president for referring to her as "the general secretary's wife", telling him that she was there as "the delegate from Barnet". It was no doubt because of her robust independence and progressive views that she became known as "Fred's Red". Although there were times when I disagreed with her views and, more often, those of her association, it was always of value to have the feelings, opinions and concerns of the union's grassroots brought home to me. In any case, as the years passed we were more often in agreement than not.

In addition to her role within the union, Anne was also active in campaigning bodies like CASE (the Campaign for the Advancement of State Education) and became a very effective member of Barnet Teachers' Council. In time Anne became chairman of the teachers' council and it was in that capacity that she became known to members of Barnet Council. It was a measure of the high regard in which she was held by the councillors that when Labour gained control of the council, with Lib Dem support, in 1994, Anne was elected chair of the education committee even though she had not been a councillor before then. It was further evidence of the esteem in which she was held that once there she was elected to chair the education committee of the Association of London Government.

In addition to her many responsibilities as a chairperson and representing the council on outside bodies, she was always unfailing in her efforts to help those who came to her with their problems and concerns. She had been like that all her life, and as a ward councillor she did even more and often with real success. She was always so involved, so much under pressure from all that she undertook, that she never had time to do much writing. Which is an enormous pity because she was a fine writer and would have had a good deal to say, not only about education and teaching, but also parenting and gardening, equality and justice, and living in France. This extract from an article she wrote for the *Times Educational Supplement* at the time of the teachers' pay strike in 1985 is a good example of Anne's sensitive yet passionate style:

> Like many other primary teachers I am a quiet militant. I share my colleagues' reluctance to take action which will affect children who are our professional *raison d'être*. We anguish equally over strike ballots and the other forms of industrial action, which affect our job satisfaction as well as the extra-curricular activities of our pupils. Yet, all over the country, the support for the union increases in quality and quantity; it is measured not only in overflowing meetings and massive rallies, but in a deep conviction that education itself is under threat. The resentment is felt by all teachers at the Government's insensitive handling of their pay claim.

She was bitterly disappointed when Labour lost control of the council in 2002 and she lost her own seat. She stood again in the next local election but was unsuccessful, and although she kept up her campaigning and remained a member of the national executive of CASE, the years of great effort on behalf of education and those in need began to take their toll. She suffered a stroke in December 2002, from which she recovered, but in 2006 she was stricken with cancer and died, courageously, in April 2007 at the North London Hospice.

At the celebration of Anne's life which we held at the Institute of Education, the then director, Geoff Whitty, said I was "clearly blessed" to have had Anne in my life. Blessed indeed, and forever deeply grateful. She was both beautiful and, in the words of *Isis,* "vividly attractive", a loving but, thankfully, not dutiful wife, tremendously support-ive, understanding and tolerant of the demands and pressures of my work and uncomplaining about the pressures of her own, a wonderful mother, courageous and adventurous, passionate and principled, a persuasive advocate and a ceaseless campaigner, a dedicated gardener, and someone who, in spite of all the demands on her time and energy, was always ready to help those in need.

Those were some of her qualities which I knew and admired because I saw them at first hand over nearly 60 years, and there were others that were seen by those who studied or trained with her, taught with her or were taught by her, worked with her in union and political activity, campaigned alongside her, served with her in local government and assorted committees and charities. Tributes to those qualities were paid in the host of letters we received after her death and by those who spoke at her celebration. The following are typical of those tributes:

"She really was the most wonderful woman. Energetic, committed, principled, caring and determined, she is such an example of how to lead a full life."

"She was a lovely, kind woman, with one of the warmest smiles I have ever seen."

"She amazed us with her endless hard work and commitment, whether it was delivering piles of papers early in the morning or fighting her corner at the town hall late in the evening."

"I can honestly say that Anne transformed my life and I will be eternally grateful to her."

In the *TES*, Roy Hattersley said Anne's death had "robbed comprehensive education of one of its most valiant champions – and thousands of children will be better for her service to education." In the *Guardian*, Geoffrey Goodman wrote that "it was, and remains, the Anne Jarvis's of this world who keep the state education system working" and that "her career as a teacher, along with her earlier research work, was altogether a remarkable record of achievement and distinction."

Having worked with such commitment in the classroom and the union and other bodies for the cause of education, Anne then had the opportunity to apply her vision and values in what became, in effect, her second career as a politician in the eight years she spent as chair of the education committee and children's committee of Barnet Council. In that capacity, Alison Moore, leader of the Labour group, said: "She was enormously popular in all schools. She made a huge contribution to developing early years education and children." And she was prepared to speak frankly and fearlessly to ministers. Estelle Morris, a former secretary of state for education, said: "She told us we had not done nearly enough. She didn't compromise. She really believed in the old-fashioned concept of public service – and never gave up." And Tim Brighouse, former commissioner for London schools, said: "She was someone who was open to argument but once her mind was made up she was never likely to be deflected from her determination to see things through."

Some days before she died, Neil and Glenys Kinnock wrote to Anne. They surely spoke for many when they said: "We know that you must be enduring spiritual as well as physical pain but we hope that the fact that huge numbers of people like us are thinking about you will be a source of strength."

Of all the many tributes paid to Anne, none was more moving than that of one of her former pupils, Ajay Kumar. He was taught by her for three years from the age of 8 to 11 at Northside School. At the celebration he said:

> I should say that I find words inadequate to share these feelings about Anne with you. Yet I hope you will gain something from these words to come.
>
> In preparing for today's event, I tried to think of what anecdotes I could share with you that gave a graphic image of Anne as a teacher. While I have many memories of my primary school days I could not find any that adequately would express what I felt Anne to be. So today I am going to talk about Anne in a more direct way.
>
> For me Anne has been one of the most important persons in my life. As my teacher and as a human being Anne inspired me from an early age to have great inquisitiveness

about the world in which I lived, to care about it, and to care about the people who inhabited it. She taught me the best way to live life as a human being.

Anne also taught me particular things, instilling in me a love of writing and of history – a history of civilisations; she instilled in me also a love of culture; most particularly a love of France, and of the French language, and of French culture. This is something that has stayed with me all my life, involving my studying, living and working in France, and visiting the country on numerous other occasions. By extension it also meant I developed a love of French culture. I think therefore it is no accident that I came to meet my wife in the South of France, in Provence, and that my wife be Italian. Ultimately Anne instilled in me a love and respect of all cultures and civilisations.

Anne's influence extended beyond schooling in the narrow sense. I was also a wayward kid and her humanity, generosity, kindness and care helped me on some kind of straight and narrow, when some of the disturbing circumstances I found myself in and some of the destructive and self-destructive forces I felt then were actually threatening to wholly derail me. At this time she displayed sensitivity and showed me a warmth, the impact and value of which I find it impossible to fully express to you today. She encouraged me to have dreams of a better life and then gave me indications of how I may achieve this.

I kept in touch with Anne after I left school and her influence on my early childhood has continued throughout my life. I feel no-one could have a better teacher and no-one could have a better friend than Anne. When I heard the news of her death I felt utmost regret that I had not been able to see more of her in recent times. I miss her terribly. I am most sorry that I could not express my gratitude to her in appropriate ways while she was alive.

Perhaps the best way I can express that gratitude now is to try to develop in myself the generosity of spirit that she had, to develop the warmth and compassion that she had and showed to other human beings, and to have something of the care she had for other people and the world as a whole.

These days I work as an artist and also a lecturer of art at Goldsmiths University of London. As a teacher I try each day to develop the qualities and skills I saw in Anne. I try to encourage, to inspire and to share with, and to listen to my students in the way that she did with me. Perhaps this is the best lesson of all.

Anne is not the past, but an ongoing present.

There could be no finer expression of what it is to be a teacher and what a teacher can do for a child than those words of Ajay. They are a further reason why Anne should and will be remembered as more than "Fred's Red" – immeasurably more.

Part 5: Where the hell is education going?

Where the hell is education going? That's a question you may well ask; I certainly do. For we are now witnessing an unprecedented fragmentation of our education system, if not its destruction. The situation was well described by my friend Professor Ron Glatter, emeritus professor of educational administration and management at the Open University, when he said: "The current extreme atomisation of the school system with its many distinct types of school, unparalleled among comparable countries internationally... is generating very large problems of both equity and manageability as well as great complexity and instability." And the zealot who is overseeing this process, and is anxious to accelerate it, is the secretary of state for education, Mr Michael Gove.

Heaven knows I've met and dealt with plenty of education ministers over the past 50 years; for some of them I had profound respect and, in some cases, friendly and constructive relations. They included a number of Tory ministers, in particular Edward Boyle, David Eccles, Keith Joseph, Kenneth Baker, Mark Carlisle and Gillian Shephard.

There are others I wouldn't rate at all. But there is one who stands out as the most irresponsible, gaffe-prone, U-turning, and the most ideological of them all – Michael Gove. Regrettably, he is also the most dangerous, given the follies he has inflicted on our education system.

I believe it is irresponsible when a secretary of state says that the GCSE is not worth the paper it is written on at a time when thousands of pupils are, often under great pressure, preparing to take it.

It is equally irresponsible to say that GCSEs in vocational subjects are "soft options" and foster the impression that head teachers who encourage their pupils to take them are doing so not for the benefit of their pupils but to improve their schools' position in the league tables.

I believe it is irresponsible for a secretary of state with responsibilities to all schools to make speeches in which he praises what he claims are the successes of academies and free schools but says nothing of the successes of community schools and primary schools.

It is irresponsible to encourage the employment of unqualified people as teachers, to be prepared to see free schools opened in closed-down shops, pubs, offices and factories in a country which once took pride in the high quality of its school architecture.

In one respect Michael Gove has excelled himself and gone beyond any of his predecessors. He has told the world that he is fighting "The Blob" in his valiant struggle to raise education standards. Not for him just the renowned "education establishment" and his "enemies of progress" – he now has "The Blob" to contend with. Such talk is not only irresponsible, it is also stupid. But if he is going to continue to indulge in it, it's about time he started to be specific about who he is accusing.

It's more than 20 years since I wrote an article challenging those who were making allegations of the responsibility of the "education establishment" for the alleged failure of our schools, colleges and universities. I never got an answer. Perhaps today it is more appropriate to ask Mr Gove who isn't part of "The Blob", for his charge seems to be so sweeping that there must be blobbers all over the place. No doubt he includes most of the teachers' unions and their members, all the university education departments, teacher educators, most researchers and professors of education (except James Tooley), the occasional think-tank, organisations like CASE, maybe some of his own department's staff, and those Ofsted inspectors whom his right-wing think-tank allies accuse of being supporters of "child-centred" education.

In addition to naming names, wouldn't it be good if he showed some desire to be as rigorous personally as he expects everybody else to be, by backing up his charges with serious evidence rather than quips aimed at catching his beloved headlines? In short: grow up Michael, it's time to be a minister.

I do not want to suggest that all the uncertainties, dangers and damage to which I refer are the sole responsibility of Michael Gove. The Lib Dems must share some of the blame. Their ministers are not slow to claim credit publicly for what they say are Lib Dem measures – in the case of education, the pupil premium and free school meals – but what do they have to say about Gove's obsession with academies and free schools, his attack on teacher education, his gaffes and U-turns on exams and the curriculum, his contempt for the teaching profession, and his fantasies over "The Blob"? These, and the growing fragmentation of the education system, have got nothing to do with reducing the national debt, the argument with which the Lib Dems seek to salve their conscience. They stem from an ideology, a belief in market forces, which one would have thought was not part of Lib Dem policy, and indeed in some respects contrary to it. So when will we hear from Mr Clegg and Mr Laws on these issues? And we don't need any more of that "It wasn't me, Guv" stuff.

Whatever bizarre arrangements the Lib Dems might make to avoid being blamed for any actions of their government which they feel may cost them votes, the fact remains that Michael Gove is their secretary of state. They are represented in his department, and they must be aware of, and they should not expect to escape some of the responsibility for, the damage, including the distortion of the work of his own department, which is being done by his ideological zeal to promote academisation and free schools and hasten the fragmentation of the education system.

Mr Gove makes statements, desperate to give the impression that what he calls for in his latest back of the envelope plan or "initiative" will be delivered, as if he only has to pull a lever in his department and it will happen. Instead of doing that he would be better advised to recognise the reality of what will actually happen in our schools. That reality was well expressed by Peter Hyman, a former aide to Tony Blair who went on to teach in three comprehensive schools. Writing in the *New Statesman* ("The Tories want to set schools back by 50 years") he said: "What politicians who look for headlines, for momentum, for a sense of 'radical reform' often fail to realise is that those on the front line are in a different game. They are not waiting for the next initiative.

"More schools spend their time subverting, adapting, ignoring and repositioning the initiatives to make them relevant and meaningful, while getting on with what they know makes the difference – improving the quality of teaching and strengthening the school's ethos. The slow and patient grind, 20, 30, 40 small things done well – that's what counts."

In the same article, Hyman was also strongly critical of Gove's attitude to the curriculum and, among other things, the abolition of the education maintenance allowance. Since he is now running a "free school" in Newham, Gove will presumably not be able to regard him as part of "The Blob". But will he listen to him?

He would also do well to take note of what Lord Puttnam had to say about mistakes made by the Labour government before the party lost the 2010 general election. Since I fervently hope Mr Gove will not be secretary of state after the next general election, I would hope his Labour successor will act on David Puttnam's remarks; but in the meantime it would be so nice if Mr Gove had a shot at learning the lessons that David offers. He certainly needs to. Lord Puttnam, speaking in the House of Lords on 7th June 2010, said:

"My own party, when in power, consistently made four mistakes. The first was to confuse initiatives with progress and to interpret each and every swallow as heralding summer. The second was that, although it talked a great deal on arrival in government about evidence-based policy making, such evidence as there was quickly became sub-sumed, or sometimes even distorted, into promoting more ideologically driven solutions. The third was to pretend to consult when in reality far-reaching decisions had already been arrived at. Experience tells me that few things infuriate intelligent people more than being cynically dragged through the motions of consultation. It is demeaning to the point of condescension and it infantilises the very people whom you are pretending to consult. Last, and to my mind most inexcusable, was the failure fully to grasp and implement what just about every piece of education research had been telling us for the past Lord knows how many years: it is the quality of classroom teaching, not changes in structure or administration, that fundamentally determines educational improvement."

It might also enable Gove to perform more like a secretary of state if, instead of blasting away at the teachers' unions as "enemies of progress", he were to participate in the world teaching summit where education ministers and the leaders of teachers' unions meet to discuss educational developments. At this year's summit, 14 ministers of education were present, including Arnie Duncan, the US education secretary. Gove attended the first summit in 2011 but has not attended since. If his colleagues from other countries can attend, why doesn't he?

In addition to his extravagant claims for the as yet unproven success of his "flagship policy", Michael Gove has sought to convince us of the success of similar policies in other countries. He cites, in particular, the success of charter schools in the USA and he used to talk of Sweden's free schools as well. Unfortunately, recent research findings in the US do not show any greater achievements by those charter schools than other public schools; and Gove has stopped talking about Sweden since some of its free schools went off the rails.

The one country he does not speak of is Finland, the country which tops the PISA tables of the OECD (the international yardstick by which the performance of schools in most countries is now measured). The reason why Gove does not refer to Finland, in spite of its acknowledged success, is that it is presumably politically inconvenient for him to do so. For Finland has no time for market forces, has no private schools, no inspection regime, far fewer examinations, a highly qualified and much respected teaching profession, no selection and no free schools.

It is worth noting that when Gove sent one of his ministers abroad to learn how children should be taught mathematics, he did not send her to nearby Finland, which tops the league for achievement, but to far-off Shanghai. Whereas in Finland there is no formal maths teaching until children are seven years old and none of the rote learning (which Gove favours) thereafter, in Shanghai children are put under great pressure, work much longer school hours, and there is extensive private tuition. Will his minister tell parents here to adopt the Shanghai model and tell them nothing about Finland?

That issue brings us to the whole question of early years in education, a subject on which the chief inspector has triggered public debate. He caused a stir when he suggested that children should start school at the age of two (or rather, that was how the media reported him), whereas what he was particularly anxious to raise was the urgent need for us to recognise that many children from poor or disadvantaged backgrounds lack the support and resources which children from more fortunate backgrounds receive. For this reason, Michael Wilshaw advocates that learning should start from the age of two and that the emphasis should be on a more formal approach rather than what he claims is the preference of the "chattering classes" for play.

I suppose it is something of a change that Wilshaw should have a go at middle class parents instead of heads and teachers, and it is not sensible to suggest that children cannot learn from play; but his main message – the need to give maximum assistance to the disadvantaged child – is surely incontestable. The coalition government has been right to introduce the pupil premium and that is not likely to be dismantled by a future government; but it has also to be recognised that overcoming disadvantage and raising achievement is a very complex matter and cannot be tackled by resources alone, vital though they are. The whole family situation of disadvantaged children has to be tackled: motivation starts with the parents' influence and assistance, which means reaching beyond the school. In this respect Wilshaw himself seems to have had a change of attitude, for in his first appearance before the Commons select committee he declared that he wanted to bring about a "no excuses" culture in schools. By that he was implying that heads and teachers were blaming the background of underachieving pupils for their failure, rather than the school, when in fact what they were doing was endorsing what he is now saying: that for most underachieving children the problem starts with the lack of the resources and encouragement which children from other backgrounds receive.

The select committee has been stressing under-achieving white working class children. The very fact that it chose to single out "white" children is interesting in itself, especially if it implies that non-white working class children are not underachieving. But there is no doubt that the whole question of disadvantage and underachievement is the biggest problem we have to tackle, and that there are no cheap and easy answers. Perhaps the pupil premium will help to some extent – if it survives the cuts and is not funded at the expense of other provision. The chief inspector has proposed that there should be a national strategy to ensure that schools in challenging areas are able to attract the best teachers, rather than the best schools grabbing the best teachers. In my opinion this is another laudable proposal, but it will not be easy to carry it out.

If it is not too much to assume that Michael Gove is sensitive enough to be embarrassed by criticism or doubts about his academies and free schools, one is entitled to think he might be embarrassed by some of the questions being asked in Parliament about his trusts. As for example when Baroness Hussein-Ece (Lib Dem) asked who the academy chains were accountable to and said that the Academies Enterprise Trust had grown to the size of a local authority and had more than 60 company directors on more than £60,000 a year.

When Ofsted carried out its first coordinated inspection of schools belonging to a single academy chain – E-ACT – it found that 11 of the chain's 16 academies had failed to provide a "good" education, including five that required "special measures"; ten of the academies had not improved since their previous inspection; four had been judged "good"; and one had been judged "outstanding". So it is not surprising that the chief inspector should want to be able to inspect the chains. It may be even less surprising that the secretary of state should be opposed to Ofsted inspecting them.

But the full extent to which Gove and his academies minister, Lord Nash, are concerned about the possible effects of Ofsted's inspections of their "flagship policy" schools, and the extent to which Gove's claims for their success are unwarranted, has been revealed by an article in the *Observer* ("Michael Gove's bid to limit fallout from failing free schools" – 5/4/14). The report deals with the content of a leaked 40-page DFE document detailing the tasks to be undertaken by Gove's newly appointed regional commissioners. Among other things, the article says:

"The document entitled 'Future Academy System – Lord Nash Session', highlights problems that new free schools are facing despite Ministers' public stance being that the program is proving a success.

"The leaked document shows that the Department for Education wants to tackle the problems at inadequate free schools before their failings are made public by Ofsted, at which point they can be used as political ammunition. It suggests that party political considerations are now driving education policy a year ahead of the General Election.

"To emphasise the importance of the new system, under which the Regional Schools Commissioners will decide who will sponsor academies among other duties, it notes that in the East Midlands and the Humber region there are 600 academies, 136 of which are under-performing. It also reveals the existence of an internal DFE grading system for the sponsors of academies such as AET, Harris and Greenwood Dale. It reveals that of the 72 sponsors in the new 'North East London and East Region' set to be monitored by a Regional Commissioner, 71% are in the two worst categories of four.

"Nationally the document notes 'Ofsted has started inspecting academies in sponsor batches – this may increase the number of sponsor under-performance issues (e.g. E-ACT) and Regional Schools Commissioners will need to work closely with each other and Ministers to deal with particularly severe issues.'"

It is, of course, true that today the majority of secondary schools have become academies, either by choice or by forced conversion. Equally, the large majority of primary schools remain community schools, in spite of the secretary of state's invitation to them to make the change. Some have changed to academy status voluntarily, others have been forced into doing so, in some cases with the DFE using an adverse Ofsted report, or the threat of one, as the weapon to secure Gove's objective.

It is equally clear that come the general election there will be a situation verging on chaos, it having emerged that the secretary of state cannot administer his "nationalised" schools from Whitehall, even with the existence of his eight regional commissioners (or should they be commissars?). As I said at the beginning of this chapter, we are witnessing a degree of fragmentation which threatens the whole system and any minister, unless he is a fanatical supporter of market forces and the end of the "system", will be faced with the need to bring back coherence. Various ideas exist about the need for a "third tier", and we have just seen the publication of a 54-page review of governance prepared by David Blunkett (former home secretary and education secretary) at the request of Tristram Hunt, Labour's current shadow education secretary. The review merits serious consideration and I suggest requires clarification on a number of issues, not least its recommendation for the appointment of directors of school standards, as to their powers and accountability. It will be necessary to see how far its proposals prove satisfactory in respect of the questions I set out below.

There can be no doubt that the next government will have to deal with the governance and growing fragmentation of the education system. I suggest that in dealing with this issue the following questions must be answered.

- Should there be an element of accountability not only to central government but to the local community as well?
- Do those who act for their community need to be democratically elected and accountable to those who elect them?
- Should the mechanism whereby we establish that element of accountability be provided through the democratic machinery that already exists, i.e. the existing local authorities, or should we create a completely new structure with a completely different set of elected representatives (not necessarily different individuals, but elected separately)?
- And would this mechanism to ensure accountability apply only to academies and free schools, or should it extend to all schools in an area, including existing community schools?
- Is there any reason, other than lack of confidence in the existing local government machinery, why the present local authorities should not be given this extended accountability function?

There are politicians who have little confidence in present-day local government and they are not confined to one political party, notwithstanding that it is their own parties that provide the majority of today's councillors. If they believe that the existing authorities are inadequate, they should address themselves to the task of ensuring that they become adequate. It is, of course, ironic that politicians say how keen they are on "localism" while pursuing policies that reduce the powers and responsibilities of local authorities, making service on them less attractive to potential officers and councillors.

Then there is the question, how successful has the voluntary or enforced change of schools to academy status been? Listening to Michael Gove one gets the impression that, in spite of the fact that most academies have been in existence for no more than three years, they are already a roaring success. He claims that "amazing things" are happening in academies and free schools (nearly all of which have been in existence for less than two years) but apparently no "amazing things" are happening in the large majority of schools that have not been "academised" or are not "free". Gove has made speeches in which he cites case after case of what he claims are highly successful schools, all of them academies or free, but makes no reference to the successes of schools which are not in those categories. Another aberration (if that is what it is) is his ability to talk about our private schools being the "best independent schools in the world" and that it is his ambition to see standards in state schools so high that you would not be able to tell the difference between a state school and a fee-paying independent school. All very laudable, but he forgets to say anything about the vast difference between the money spent on children in state schools and the fees paid for education in the private sector.

There is another conflict between what Gove claims to be the success of the academies and their "amazing things" and what has been said by witnesses appearing before the House of Commons select committee. Reporting on one session of the committee, *Education Journal* (24/3/14) said: "The panel [of expert witnesses] agreed that the academies program was still at an early stage and that it was too early to make firm conclusions." Hardly an endorsement of Michael Gove's bombast. Equally embarrassing will be the Ofsted reports on failing academies and free schools. One individual report may not sink his flagship policy but it will not have helped.

In my experience as a school governor, one of the main concerns of parents is the quality of their children's teachers. That is completely understandable (though I find it surprising that so many commentators and politicians have taken so long to appreciate that the quality of the teaching in classrooms is central to the performance and achievement of pupils). Yet the present secretary of state, having at an early stage called for higher entry qualifications for those wishing to become teachers, is prepared to allow the employment of unqualified people in academies and free schools.

Gove has supported the establishment of a College or Institute of Teaching, but the context in which he expressed that support – an attack on the teaching unions – suggests that he sees such an institution as a means of undermining the influence of the unions. What he may not recognise is that, if a College of Teaching were to be established (and the teachers' unions support that), one of the first declarations it would be likely to make would be an insistence on the need for high quality qualifications for all teachers.

It is high time that Michael Gove abandoned his willingness to allow the employment of unqualified persons in any publicly financed school. He should also abandon his attempt to alter the whole basis for the education and training of teachers. What he is doing in this respect is as damaging as the fragmentation he is causing in the education system itself. It is producing what Charlie Taylor, the head of the National College of Leadership (appointed by Michael Gove), has said is "causing instability and turbulence in the system". Gove's policy of providing most of the education of intending teachers by what is known as Schools Direct and, to a lesser extent, Teach First, is leading to the closure of education departments in a growing number of universities. This will have serious consequences for the standing and output of teachers. It will also lead to a considerable imbalance in areas which will provide opportunities for teacher education in the "teaching schools" which Mr Gove wants to assume a key role in teacher education: but they are not spread evenly around the country. It is also questionable how far universities outside a favoured minority will be engaged in teacher education, yet the link with the universities is surely crucial to the professional status of teachers. In Finland, where teachers enjoy the highest professional status of any country in the world, there are "teaching schools", but they are totally incorporated in their universities.

There are two other issues where there is uncertainty and about which questions need to be asked – and answered. The first relates to selection, which could well become an issue at the next general election. The populist UKIP has declared its support for the reintroduction of grammar schools and there have been reports of increasingly noisy calls from Tory MPs for more grammar schools. Doubtless those calls could increase if Tory MPs fear they could lose their seats to UKIP in the general election. Michael Gove has also expressed support for grammar schools, and Boris Johnson's recent flirtation with eugenics suggests he might go down the same path. In his time, John Major, when prime minister, raised the idea of a grammar school in every town, but then dropped it. If Gove tries to revive the idea, he would, as reported, be on a collision course with the chief inspector. Sir Michael Wilshaw has made what was classed as a "scathing assault" on England's 164 state-funded grammar schools. In the wake of a recent OECD report on school standards, Sir Michael said: "Grammar schools are stuffed full of middle class kids. A tiny percentage are on free school meals: 3%. That is a nonsense. Anyone who thinks grammar schools are going to increase social mobility needs to look at those figures. I don't think they work... What we have to do is make sure all schools do well in the areas in which they are located."

Wilshaw will not get any thanks from Gove for those remarks, any more than David Willetts did for saying something similar several years ago. Given the extent to which forms of selective school are emerging in some areas in spite of the admissions code, it is important to ask what effort the politicians are going to make to end selection throughout the country as a step towards achieving the world-class education system they profess to want.

There are some politicians who are now saying that what we should be concerned about is "standards not structures". As Ron Glatter says: "Talking about teaching quality – though there are controversies involved – is less contentious than structural issues, so there is temptation to play the latter down to avoid becoming embroiled in too much conflict." But to think that talking only about teaching quality will enable politicians to dodge the bullets of the *Daily Mail* and other right-wing newspapers is an illusion. Of course it is necessary to talk about teaching quality and what happens in the classroom. But it is also necessary to talk about structures, for they determine what kind of education and the variety of opportunities we will provide for future generations.

Politicians should also be asked what they intend to do about the future financing of access to higher education. We now have a system of student loans that leaves most of them faced with substantial debts when they finish their studies. The politicians told them they didn't have to worry because they would not have to start repaying their loans until they achieved a certain level of salary. What the politicians did not spell out was that at the same time the government was making substantial cuts in aspects of university funding which they were expecting would be restored by the substantially higher fees that students would be charged, rather than funded by the taxpayer.

The whole scheme has run into major difficulty because the students have not been repaying their loans on anything like the scale the government anticipated. The House of Commons public accounts committee has warned that the government has consistently over-estimated annual repayments of student loans and consistently under-estimated the debt that will never be repaid. It has been said that the current £45bn of outstanding student loans on the government's books would rise dramatically to £200bn by 2042. So the question to be faced is: should fees be raised even higher, should the repayment of loans start at a lower salary level, or should it be recognised that quality higher and further education provision makes a vital contribution to our economy and our society and should the cost therefore be met by the taxpayer?

Having considered that difficult question, one has to recognise that there are other major questions that we all have to face, not least the vital and increasingly costly questions of social care and child care, and that takes us on to considering what kind of society we want – but that is a subject for somebody else's book, not this one.

I could have raised certain other intriguing questions, such as the plotting or non-plotting against the chief inspector, who told the *Sunday Times* that he was "spitting blood" over the ideas of right-wing think-tanks, including one founded by Michael Gove, aimed at stopping Ofsted from inspecting academies and free schools, and accusing some

Ofsted inspectors of supporting "child centred" education. But that would be approaching the realm of crime fiction, and that's not for this book either. The subsequent statement by Michael Wilshaw to the education select committee, that he had not agreed with Gove's decision not to reappoint Lady Sally Morgan as chairman of Ofsted, only added to the sense of intrigue in high places.

Before signing off, I have one further thought. Since this chapter began by asking where education is going, I suggest there is another question the politicians should be asked, and it relates to an aspect of education which is too easily dismissed.

There is, understandably, considerable and increasing discussion of our country's ageing population, and it is essential that the question of social care is faced. But should we not also discuss the need to see education as a life-long process, and that many of us would benefit greatly from bigger efforts to provide for our minds as well as our bodies?

There are already a number of organisations which are doing excellent work, like the University of the Third Age and, of course, the Open University; and there are many local organisations which promote a host of opportunities for activities with an educational aspect, and the new technologies make these more accessible. It is commendable that so much of this kind of activity is undertaken willingly on a voluntary basis and with limited resources. But rarely is attention given to the need for a bigger collective effort to make public provision for education for the increasing numbers who are benefiting from the interests that those in the Third Age will surely have and wish to pursue.

I'm aware that, given my age, this might sound like special pleading, but I do think it would be a good thing if politicians, and others, would get around to recognising that learning is a life-long process and that catering for it is every bit as important as providing, at enormous cost, railways that will enable us to reach Birmingham and other big cities half an hour quicker than we used to. Spending a billion or two to speed up our minds might also help us to put the half-hours we've saved to good use.

To conclude on a more uplifting note, I would draw attention to the works of Pasi Sahlberg, the former chief inspector of schools in Finland. He has written an excellent book, *Finnish Lessons,* which Michael Gove would profit from reading (I hope). At a meeting at the Royal Society of Arts (April 2014) he was asked how Finland had achieved its undoubted success in education. He replied that the five factors that contributed to Finland's educational success were:

- Collaboration not competition.
- Less confrontation between teachers and society.
- Less emphasis on "starting early".
- Less accountability and more trust.
- Less school choice and a greater emphasis on equity.

That is a set of tests which Michael Gove and his policies would fail. We need a secretary of state who would pass them.

Lightning Source UK Ltd.
Milton Keynes UK
UKOW02f1924040914

238111UK00001B/14/P